A Feminist Perspective on the Novels of Shashi Deshpande

The present book seeks to present Shashi Deshpande as a feminist writer focussing on her novels. It reveals Deshpande's instinctive ability to articulate the feelings of the contemporary, urban, educated upper-middle-class woman who is caught in the transitional period between tradition and modernity. It shows how co-operating within the framework of a male-dominated and tradition-bound society, Deshpande's heroines are conscious of their predicament as victims of inequity.

for
my husband
Sri C. Vijayashekhar Reddy

A Feminist Perspective on the Novels of Shashi Deshpande

Y.S. SUNITA REDDY

PRESTIGE

Published by
PRESTIGE BOOKS
3/28, East Patel Nagar
New Delhi 110 008
e-mail: prestigebooks@greatindian.com

ISBN: 81-7551-103-6

Rs. 500
Prestige Books
International

Composed by Vivek Mathur, Delhi 110 006 Ph. 3981867
Printed at Chaman Offset Press, New Delhi 110 002

Contents

Preface

Though Shashi Deshpande has emerged as a leading woman novelist on the Indian literary horizon, and won the prestigious Sahitya Akademi Award for her novel, *That Long Silence*, she has not received the critical attention she deserves. The only book, *The Image of Woman in the Novels of Shashi Deshpande* by Sarabjit Sandhu, that has been published so far gives only a brief account of the image of woman, the study being confined to the early novels of Deshpande. Barring a few articles in some journals and books, there is no full-length study of Shashi Deshpande's fiction especially from the feminist perspective. Hence the need for a close study of Shashi Deshpande's novels as products of feminism which offers a fresh perspective for critical analysis, linking literature with real life situations.

The aim of the present book is to evaluate the novels of Shashi Deshpande from a feminist perspective. Deshpande has gained reputation as a serious writer with tremendous potential. Most of Deshpande's protagonists are women who are educated and exposed to Western ideas. The emotional upheavals in the minds of these women and their reactions to various issues related to women, caught between tradition and modernity, are susceptible to treatment from a feminist angle.

The woman of today stands poised on the threshold of social change in an unenviable position. She is intensely aware of the injustice heaped on her and unlike her counterpart a generation ago, she does not believe that woman is an inferior being who must remain passive and submissive. This awakening of the woman's consciousness as delineated by Shashi Deshpande in her novels deserves a close study to assess the extent of articulation of a woman's point of view. Hence the need for a close study of

Shashi Deshpande's novels as products of feminism which offers a fresh perspective for critical analysis linking literature with real life situations.

The book is divided into nine chapters. The introductory chapter traces the origin, growth and development of feminism in the literary world, in general, and in Indian writing in English, in particular. Deshpande's view of feminism is studied while tracing the formative influences on her writing.

The second chapter unravels the protagonist, Indu's attempt to assert herself in the novel, *Roots and Shadows*. It records the suffocation experienced by Indu in a society governed by the age-old customs and traditions. It also unmasks the protagonist of her garb of a liberated woman and exposes the hypocrisy of ostensibly progressive-minded men like Jayant, Indu's husband.

The third chapter unveils the fragility of the male ego which refuses to accept an inferior in marriage in the novel *The Dark Holds No Terrors*. Through the life of the protagonist, Saru, Deshpande highlights the trauma of a woman who is made the victim of her husband's frustrations because economically and socially she has achieved a superior status. The chapter also seeks to discuss the gender discrimination practised by parents towards their children.

The fourth chapter concerns itself with the protagonist Jaya's passage through a maze of uncertainty and apprehension towards the assertion of her self in the novel, *That Long Silence*. It reveals the trauma of an ostensibly contented housewife who is smothered under the weight of male-dominance.

The fifth chapter discusses Deshpande's fourth novel *The Binding Vine*, in which the author makes an attempt to venture into an area—the issue of marital rape—which, perhaps, has not been dealt with by any other Indian writer in English. It focusses attention on the victims of man's lust and woman's helplessness.

The sixth chapter is a study of Deshpande's fifth novel, *A Matter of Time*, which is different in theme and presentation from her earlier novels. In this novel, the author makes a successful attempt to present the story from the point of view of her male protagonist, thereby fulfilling her self-confessed desire to write of human beings and not of men or women.

The seventh chapter is concerned with Shashi Deshpande's sixth and most recent novel *Small Remedies* which is a sensitive portrayal of women's quest for identity in a partiarchal world.

The eighth chapter deals with Deshpande's technique and style in presenting her thematic concerns. The narrative technique she employs, her use of myth, satire and irony and her handling of the language are discussed.

The concluding chapter offers a summing-up of the book highlighting the feminist perspective in the novels of Deshpande. Operating within the framework of a male-dominated and tradition-bound society, Deshpande's heroines are conscious of their predicament as victims of inequality. It is shown that Deshpande's depiction of her protagonists is realistic to the core inasmuch as she does not succumb to the temptation of creating exceptionally strong women characters who revolt against conventional morality. Deshpande seems to write about the middle-class Indian women and their feelings, not as their champion but as their articulator.

I take this opportunity to express my deep sense of gratitude to Prof. K. Venkata Reddy, Professor of English, S.K. University, Anantapur, for having initiated me into Shashi Deshpande's fiction, and what is more, provided the necessary guidance and help to complete my work. I am also grateful to his wife, Dr. N.E. Bhagyavathy, for the warm hospitality she has always extended to me.

I would like to acknowledge the support and encouragement of my husband, children and parents-in-law, and thank them for putting up with much inconvenience during the preparation of my book. I am greatly indebted to my parents, Mr. Y.S. Anand Reddy and Dr. Y. Susheela Reddy, for their constant support and encouragement without which I would never have completed this task. I am deeply beholden to my mother who is the moving spirit behind my research work.

I would also like to thank Mrs. O. Vijayalakshmi for instilling confidence in me with constant words of encouragement; Prem and Sreedevi for extending their cooperation in securing proper material for my research; Mr. George Bhaskar for urging me to pursue my studies further and for going through my book, offering suggestions; and my friend, Sandhya, for her affectionate help.

I am indeed grateful to my uncle and aunt, Prof. C. Venkata Reddy and Smt. Sulochana for their hospitality and cooperation.

Y.S. SUNITA REDDY

Introduction

It is a truth universally acknowledged that women, who are physically and mentally equipped to perform on par with men, have not only been denied existence as complete human beings, but also deprived of the opportunity to give expression to their feelings, their thoughts and their anguish. As Sushila Singh puts it: "Human experience for centuries has been synonymous with the masculine experience with the result that the collective image of humanity has been one-sided and incomplete. Woman has not been defined as a subject in her own right but merely has an entity that concerns man either in his real life or his fantasy life."[1] The feminist movement, which started in the West in the 1960s, went a long way in arresting the injustice meted out to women. There had been an abundance of feminist writing which preceded and followed this movement, but there is much still left to be done to wipe out the age-old prejudices and misconceptions regarding women.

The term 'feminism' was first used by the nineteenth century French dramatist, Alexander Dumas, to refer to the then-emerging movement for women's rights which was mostly limited to politics. It gradually spread across the world, securing complete rights for women—political, social, economic and educational. In the later part of the twentieth century, it swept across the world, shaking it out of its centuries-old complacency, making people think anew about age-old beliefs. In India, a population steeped in religious beliefs, superstition and tradition did not readily get influenced by this movement. The *Manu Smriti*, which has been widely accepted in India as a text laying down the rules of social behaviour, declares:

> Day and night, women must be kept in subordination to the

> males of the family: in childhood to the father, in youth to her husband, in old age to her sons. . . . Even though the husband be destitute of virtue and seeks pleasure elsewhere, he must be worshipped as God.[2]

Feminism, thus, plays little or no part in the lives of most Indians. A few Indian writers in English have attempted to challenge the age-old myths surrounding the man-woman relationship. Some have succeeded in their attempt, if not in finding an ideal solution, but, at least in creating an awareness of the existing inequalities in society.

According to the historian Linda Gordan, feminism is "an analysis of women's subordination for the purpose of figuring out how to change it."[3] Women constitute roughly half the world's population, but their contribution in various fields of activity has been totally disproportionate to their numerical strength. Branded as the weaker sex they have been denied full justice—social, economic and political. An awareness of the inequalities present in society resulted in the Women's Liberation Movement as late as the mid-nineteenth century. The credit for providing an impetus to such a movement must certainly go to pioneers like Simone de Beauvoir, who sought to shatter the myth of femininity in her book, *The Second Sex*. First published in French in the year 1949, it was later translated into English making it accessible to the rest of the world. With a frankness hitherto unheard of, she writes:

> All agree in recognising the fact that female exists in the human species; today as always they make up about one-half of humanity. And yet we are told that femininity is in danger; we are exhorted to be women, remain women, become women. It would appear, then, that every female human being is not necessarily a woman; to be so considered she must share in that mysterious and threatened reality known as femininity. Is this attribute something secreted by the ovaries? Or is it a platonic essence, a product of the philosophic imagination.[4]

Simone de Beauvoir draws heavily on various disciplines like biology, psychology and history to express her ideas clearly. She studies in detail issues like a girl's education, marriage, prostitution, and domestic chores which she describes as unpaid drudgery. She discusses frankly topics which were hitherto considered to be taboo—sexual initiation and sexual pleasure for women. She also seeks to debunk the sentimental propaganda about maternity.

Though Beauvoir's book sowed the seeds for a revolution, it did not exactly initiate the Women's Movement. The book which sparked off the Movement was Betty Friedan's *The Feminine Mystique*, published in 1963. Fifteen years after graduating from college, Friedan conducted interviews with many of her erstwhile classmates and the results of this survey proved that the general assumption of a woman achieving happiness and contentment in marriage and motherhood was false. Most of the women interviewed by Friedan were wives and mothers, ostensibly blessed with all the comforts of life. Yet the survey proved that they were merely playing the role of a devoted wife and loving mother and were supposed to seek fulfilment in it. Friedan holds the view:

> For a woman, as for a man, the need for self-fulfilment—autonomy, self-realisation, independence, individuality, self-actualisation—is as important as the sexual need, with as serious consequences when it is thwarted. Women's sexual problems are, in this sense, by-products of the suppression of her basic need to grow and fulfil her potentialities as a human being, potentialities which the mystique of feminine fulfilment ignores.[5]

Friedan's book was followed by Kate Millett's *Sexual Politics* in 1969. Millett is considered to be another important feminist of the twentieth century. She vociferously argues that in the patriarchal society, woman has been accorded a demeaning position. She gives a graphic explanation of the insecurities faced by woman and she anticipates the problem which society would face one day in the form of female foeticide with the result of rapid scientific development which would enable pre-natal sex determination tests. She says:

> The gnawing suspicion that plagues any minority member, that myths propagated about his inferiority might after all be true often reaches remarkable proportions in the personal insecurities of women. Some find their subordinate position so hard to bear that they repress and deny its existence. But a large number will recognise and admit their circumstances when they are properly phrased. Of two studies which asked women if they would have preferred to be born male, one found that one fourth of one sample admitted as much, and in another sample, one half, when inquired of children, who have not yet developed as serviceable techniques of evasion, what this choice might be, if they had one, the answers of female children in a large majority of cases clearly favour birth into the elite group, whereas boys overwhelmingly reject the option of being girls. The phenomenon of parents' prenatal preferences for male issue is too common to require much elaboration. In the light of the imminent possibility of parents actually choosing the sex of their child, such a tendency is becoming the cause of some concern in scientific circles.[6]

Propagating the same brand of militant feminism, Germaine Greer feels that marriage as an institution must be abolished because, "If women are to affect a significant amelioration in their condition it seems obvious that they must refuse to marry."[7]

The Women's Movement also produced a number of feminist novelists. Sylvia Plath's *Bell Jar* took American women by storm. The novel depicts the transformation of the young, innocent and oppressed heroine, Esther, into a vengeful Diana. The novelist uses the exquisitely handcrafted mat made by Mrs. Willard, one of the characters in the book, to symbolise the oppression of women. This mat is not used for interior decoration as some object of art but rather as a kitchen mat to be soiled under the feet of Mr. Willard. It makes Esther think: "And I knew that in spite of all the roses and kisses and restaurant dinners a man showered on a woman before he married her, what he secretly wanted when the wedding service ended was for her to flatten out under his feet like Mrs. Willard's kitchen mat."[8]

Other feminist novelists in the West like Margaret Drabble, Doris Lessing, Iris Murdoch, Marilyn French and Margaret Atwood have created a niche for themselves in the literature produced in this century. They have come a long way from the handicaps and constraints faced by their counterparts two hundred years ago. Women in those days did not dare defy the rigid norms laid down by society. While it was permissible for men to ignore social decorum and prudish notions of morality, a woman writer was expected to restrict herself only to certain areas of life. Even such writing was possible only after much sacrifice. Writing about women writers, Anne Stevenson comments:

> It is surprising how many spinster writers there have been: Jane Austen, Emily Bronte, Stevie Smith, Charlotte Mew, Mananne Moore, Elizabeth Bishop. These women may have suffered, but they suffered as women whc attempted neither to fight male domination nor compromise themselves to suit it. Theirs was a narrow independence, even a selfish one, but it was real. It was bought at the price of what used to be called 'Womanliness'—sex, marriage, children and the socially acceptable position of a wife.[9]

Society has undergone a great change since then. No longer do women writers have to assume psuedonyms, as in the case of George Eliot, to shield their identity. Women writers today enjoy a relatively greater measure of freedom and do not hesitate to explore regions of experience which were earlier considered taboo. Even in a conservative nation like India, we now have Shobha De who has dared to enter the exclusively male domain of pornography and become a commercial success.

In general, however, western feminists far outnumber their Indian counterparts and are a lot more stridently feminist in their approach. In India, the first generation of Indian writers in English—Mulk Raj Anand, R.K. Narayan and Raja Rao missed out a great opportunity. A wealth of material in the form of the freedom struggle and the women involved in it seemed to have escaped their notice. Anand, obviously, had been too deeply involved in championing the cause of the underdog in society to pay attention to the travails of women. His protagonist Gauri in *The Old Woman and the Cow*, however, is a fine example of his idea of women's emancipation. However, at least some of Narayan's women characters of everyday life try to assert themselves in their desire for a career or their need for physical gratification. If he has portrayed the meek and submissive woman in Margayya's wife in his novel *The Financial Expert* and Savitri in *The Dark Room*, he has also created vibrant and sometimes radical women characters like Daisy and Rosie in his novels, *The Painter of Signs* and *The Guide* respectively. These heroines, however, are not role models whose experiences are meant to be emulated. Talking of Daisy, Shanta Krishnaswamy says: "She is unique in that she is able to cast aside all culturally imposed feelings of guilt and shame on womanhood and sex. Narayan, however, in depriving her of personal fulfilment in marriage and domesticity, warns us about the excesses of rampant feminism which would lead to a destructive or deathlike androgynous blurring of the two sexes."[10]

The women in Raja Rao's fiction are reduced to mere automatons. Those of his women characters who aspire for more, end up feeling bitter like Saroja or settle for passivity like Savitri, dutifully playing her role as the wife of a government officer in *The Serpent and the Rope*. The women in his novels are victims of domestic injustice and tyrannical tradition, but he proposes no solution to their dilemma. This may be because as Shanta Krishnaswamy says, "The culture he springs from and which he has imbibed so thoroughly in his entire being, precludes Rao from resolving the woman's issue in concrete terms." (vi) In Bhabani Bhattacharya's novels, woman is the epitome of all virtues and plays an important role in bringing about social reform. But in spite of being pure and noble, she is victimised.

Kajoli in *So Many Hungers!* reveals an unconquerable spirit in the face of endless suffering and misery. The city-bred Mohini in *Music for Mohini* transforms the village, Behula, symbolic of a country steeped in superstition and obsolete customs, into a model village with the help of her progressive-minded husband. However, it may be said that "the picture he paints of the woman is idyllic, tender and charming, sometimes even too optimistic to be realistic. (353)

Thus, while writing about women, men tend to go to extremes—either highlighting their weaknesses or deifying them and putting them on a pedestal, making the characters seem unreal. Women writers, on the other hand, are more honest in their portrayal of women in their novels. Kamala Markandaya very successfully portrays the double pulls that the Indian woman is subjected to—between her desire to assert her dignity as human being and her duty as a daughter, wife and mother. She also points out how the distortions in the economic and social order affect women more than men. Through her protagonist Rukmani in *Nectar in a Sieve*, she proves that within the traditional role, she can accommodate her other roles as a human being, and not through alienation and self-laceration, but through expansion and communion a deeper self-knowledge can be attained. Another example is Sarojini in *A Silence of Desire*, who is determined to overcome her problems in her own way. It is perhaps only in *Possession* that Markandaya transforms the traditionally suppressed woman into a domineering and tyrannical possessor. In most of her other novels, however, the woman is a source of dormant strength and shores up the male protagonist from collapse.

Anita Desai explores the disturbed psyche of the modern Indian women. Her protagonists are usually highly intelligent and sensitive women who end up exhausted and on the verge of mental crises in their attempt to manage a home and children and find emotional fulfilment. They usually resort to drastic steps when their predicament reaches a climax. Maya in *Cry, the Peacock* is a highly sensitive, caring woman bound in marriage to the practical, down-to-earth lawyer Gautama, who remains totally oblivious to his wife's emotional needs. Physically and emotionally, her body and mind crave for attention, the denial of which leads to dire consequences with Gautama being pushed to his death by her. *Where Shall We Go This Summer?* describes the gnawing void in the life of Sita by reviewing her life as a woman, wife and mother. It is an intense story of a middle-aged woman torn between her desire to abandon her comfortable, albeit boring, existence and the realisation that the bonds that bind her to it cannot easily be broken. Desai, in all her novels, presents the predicament of sensitive women characters, who find it very difficult to adjust themselves in the present mechanical and urbanised set up. She, however, makes no attempt to find solutions to their various problems.

Ruth Prawer Jhabvala is mostly preoccupied with the travails of the white woman in India. She writes predominantly from her own viewpoint with her bitter experiences in an alien land. Her portrayal of women is very limited and narrow, and provokes Shanta Krishnaswamy to comment that "her examples of women in her fiction seem to make people unacquainted with India believe that all Indian women are contemptible, flighty or neurotic and pathetic creatures." (356)

Nayantara Sahgal, another prominent Indian woman writer, started writing before the feminist movement was launched in the sixties. Yet she has dealt with problems concerning women which went on to become major issues in the feminist movement. She writes sensitively of the way women suffer owing to sexist bias in a partriachal set-up. In *The Day in Shadow*, she gives a sensitive account of the suffering of a woman in Indian society when she chooses to divorce her husband. The protagonist Simrit feels diminished and humiliated not only by the stigma attached to divorce but also by the cruel 'consent terms' of the divorce which compel her to pay a staggering amount of tax on an income she cannot even use. The novel, however, cannot be labelled feminist because Simrit, in spite of her liberated way of thinking, does not have the courage to stand without male support. If it is not her husband Som, it is Raj, who she later depends on to solve her problems. In *Rich Like Us*, Ram inflicts great emotional violence on both his wives Mona and Rose. Though both the women are aware of the injustice done to them, habit makes them willing victims of exploitation and injustice. Sahgal, it must be observed, works out her feminist ideas in a limited world. She usually restricts herself to the study of women of one class—the elite. She makes a close and sensitive study of the sufferings of the women of this class and shows how they refuse to remain chained to their subordinate roles and how they defy traditional norms in search of emancipation. Most of her works, however, also deal with the impersonal world of politics in a story running parallel to the main theme of the personal world of man-woman relationships.

Though not an avowed feminist, Shashi Deshpande occupies a significant place among the contemporary women novelists who concern themselves with the problems of women and their quest for identity. Deshpande's creative talent and accomplishment have established her credentials as a worthy successor and contemporary to the writers mentioned above. Her protagonists are modern, educated young women, crushed under the weight of a male-dominated and tradition-bound society. Her attempt to give an honest portrayal of their sufferings, disappointments and frustrations makes her novels susceptible to treatment from the feminist angle. She, however, maintains that her novels are not intended to be read as feminist texts. This is evident from what she says: "A woman who writes of women's experiences often brings in some aspects of those experiences that have angered her, roused her strong feelings. I don't see why this has to be labelled feminist fiction."[11]

Ibsen, who heralded the idea of woman's emancipation with his character, Nora, in *A Doll's House*, also disclaims any connection with women's rights. In a banquet held in his honour by the Norwegian Society for Women's Rights, he says: "Of course, it is incidentally desirable to solve the problem of women; but that has not been my whole object. My task has been the portrayal of human beings."[12]

While it may not have been Deshpande's intention to propound any particular theory, even a cursory reading of her novels displays a tremendous amount of sympathy for women. Most of her protagonists are educated and exposed to western ideas. As Ramamoorthy puts it, "Her heroines speak of Virginia Woolf's *A Room of One's Own* and Betty Friedan and it becomes obvious that the women she has created are feminists if she is not one."[13] Moreover, the attitudes and reactions of her protagonists to various issues related to women who are caught between tradition and modernity do provide ample material for treatment from a feminist angle.

A reading of Shashi Deshpande's novels reveals a deep understanding of the female psyche particularly that of the educated, urban, middle-class woman. Deshpande is undoubtedly an outstanding Indian English novelist with four volumes of short stories, four children's books and six novels to her credit. She was born and brought up in Dharwad, Karnataka, and is the daughter of the renowned Kannada dramatist and Sanskrit scholar, Sriranga, who is described as the Bernard Shaw of Kannada theatre. She graduated in Economics from Elphinstone College, Bombay and in Law from the Government Law College, Bangalore. Much later, she took a post-graduate degree in English from the Mysore University. She married Dr. Deshpande, a neuro-pathologist in 1962 and the initial years of her marriage were largely given over to bringing up her two sons. Recounting the influences in her life, Shashi Deshpande says: "There are three things in my early life that have shaped me as a writer. These are: That my father was a writer, that I was educated exclusively in English and that I was born a female."[14]

In an interview to Vanamala Vishwanath, Shashi Deshpande says that she began writing most casually and without any intention of settling down to a career in writing. She had accompanied her husband, a commonwealth scholar, to England and lived there for a year. In order not to forget her experiences in England, she began writing them down. The fact that they were found worthy of being published, encouraged her to try a career in journalism. A stint at *Onlooker* further encouraged her to try her hand at short stories and, in a sudden burst of creativity, she wrote several short stories which were published in reputed magazines and which were later compiled into four volumes. Her first collection of short stories *The Legacy*, published in 1972, was prescribed for the graduate students in Columbia University. Other collections of short stories are *It Was Dark*, *The Miracle* and *It Was the Nightingale*. In between, Shashi Deshpande also tried her hand at detective writing and wrote three detective serials, two of which were subsequently expanded and published as regular novels—*Come Up and Be Dead* and *If I Die Today*. The racy style of narration made these books quite popular but Deshpande herself considers them failures.

A close study of Deshpande's short stories and novels reveals an author who is intelligent, articulate and relatively free from prejudices regarding gender, but at the same time highly sensitive to the issues involving women. The relentless probing of man-woman relationship by the author intrigues the reader enough to question her stand on feminism. Deshpande is perhaps the only Indian author who has made a bold attempt to give voice to the frustrations and disappointments of women despite her vehement denial of being a feminist.

Roots and Shadows is the first full length novel written by Deshpande though it was published after *The Dark Holds No Terrors*, her second novel. The novel highlights the agony and suffocation experienced by the protagonist Indu in a male-dominated and tradition-bound society. She finds herself alienated when she refuses to conform to the rigid code laid down by society. Marriage to the man of her choice brings only disillusionment when she finds her educated and ostensibly progressive-minded husband no different from the average Indian male. She is even contemptuous of herself when she realises that she has all along been unconsciously aping the model of the ideal Indian wife. The novel gains its feminist stance from Indu's persistent exploration of herself as an individual. An extra-marital affair helps her to break free from the emotional bondage of matrimony and makes her aware of herself and realise that it is possible to exercise autonomy within the parameters of marriage. *Roots and Shadows* also offers us scope to observe meaningless rituals and customs all of which help to perpetuate the myth of male superiority. Seen through the novelist's eye, insignificant everyday details take on a new dimension and highlight the gross inequalities present in society.

Deshpande's second novel, *The Dark Holds No Terrors*, seeks to discuss the male ego which refuses to accept a secondary position in marriage. The novel narrates the harrowing experience of the protagonist, Saru, who enjoys a greater economic and social status than her husband Manohar. The trauma of being the victim of her husband's frustration which manifests itself in the form of sexual sadism is vividly portrayed. Deshpande also makes the readers aware of society's reaction to the superior status of the wife in a marriage, which leads the husband to develop an inferiority complex. The novel also seeks to discuss the blatant gender discrimination which is shown even by parents towards their daughters. Deshpande effectively conveys the craving by parents for a male child and the disastrous effect it can have on a sensitive young girl. Denied of parental love and victim of her husband's frustrations, Saru undergoes an arduous journey into herself and liberates herself from guilt, shame and humiliation to emerge in full control over her life.

Deshpande's third novel, *That Long Silence*, brought her into limelight as it was published by the British feminist publishing house, Virago. The novel deals with the protagonist Jaya's passage through a maze of self-doubts and fears towards the affirmation of herself. A crisis in the middle-class family of the protagonist triggers off a chain of events which compel her to view her life in retrospection. What follows is an honest and frank account of Jaya's life. In her anxiety to play the role of wife and mother to perfection, Jaya realises that she does not do justice to her talents as a writer. Her constant fear of displeasing her husband and inviting the censure of society, not only make her give up writing but also discourage her from acknowledging her friendship with a man who is not her husband, brother or father.

Jaya is representative of the modern young woman—educated and aware—nevertheless unable to break free from the stranglehold of tradition. In the process of telling her story, she offers us a glimpse into the lives of ostensibly content housewives who are nevertheless suppressed under the weight of male dominance. Deshpande, however, avoids the facile solution of laying the blame on men alone and tries to view the man-woman relationship objectively. She observes through her novel that both men and women, being products of their culture, find it difficult to outgrow the images and roles allotted to them by society.

In her fourth novel, *The Binding Vine*, Deshpande uses the personal tragedy of the narrator/protagonist Urmi to focus attention on victims like Kalpana and Mira—victims of man's lust and woman's helplessness. The novelist makes a bold attempt to portray the agony of a wife who is the victim of marital rape—a theme which perhaps has not been touched upon by any other Indian writer in English. Urmi tries to reconstruct the pathetic story of a bright and attractive girl, Mira, who wrote poems in the solitude of an unhappy marriage to alleviate her suffering. Urmi also crusades for the cause of another victim, Kalpana, who is brutally raped and is on her death bed. The novelist deftly handles the juxtaposition of the two situations—rape committed within the precincts of marriage and outside it. The novelist gives a moving account of the plight of women raped outside marriage, who would rather suffer in silence than be exposed to the humiliation involved in publicising the event and that of married women whose bodies are violated by their legally wedded husbands but who would never dare reveal this to anyone. They would rather stifle their voice of protest for the sake of social and moral security. Deshpande, through the voice of Urmi, also offers us a glimpse into the lives of myriad other women, who are ostensibly more liberated than their predecessors but, who, nevertheless, are victims of some form of violence or deprivation.

In her novel, *A Matter of Time*, Deshpande liberates herself from the narrow confines of women and their problems and enters into the metaphysical world of philosophy. The novel is essentially the story of three women from three generations from the same family and how they cope with the tragedy that overwhelms them. But in narrating their story a greater emphasis has been placed on Gopal, the perpetrator of this tragedy, and his view of life.

Shashi Deshpande's latest novel, *Small Remedies* is the most confident assertion of her strength as a novelist with her deliberate denial of sentimentality and her total control over the unwieldy material. Structured as a biography within a biography, it is about Savitribai Indorekar, the ageing doyenne of Hindustani music, who denies a marriage and a home with a view to pursuing her genius. It also tells the story of Leela, who gives up her respectability in order to gain love and unhappiness in equal measure. At the centre of this sprawling narrative is Madhu who, in telling the stories of Savitribai, Leela and Munni, hopes to find a way out of her own despair.

Come Up and Be Dead and *If I Die Today*, two of Deshpande's detective serials which have been expanded and published as novels have not been included for study in this book because the very nature of their themes is totally at variance with the subject of this study. Shashi Deshpande's interest in detective fiction is obvious from her review of *A Woman's Eye: New Stories by the Best Women Crime Writers*. Her remarkably sagacious assessment of the stories leaves one in no doubt about her love for the genre. But a reading of both her detective novels drives home the point that to review a book and to write one are two entirely different things. The books are at best amateurish as Deshpande herself has acknowledged.

Come Up and Be Dead has been compared unfavourably with Agatha Christie's *Cat among the Pigeons* by one reviewer, because the setting for both novels is a girls' school where a series of murders take place. The novel which starts briskly enough falters towards the middle and is unable to hold the reader's interest in the true tradition of a whodunit. *If I Die Today* is set in the resident quarters of a large charity hospital where again there are a series of killings beginning with the murder of the terminally in patient Guru. The vast number of characters in the area, their frustrations and disappointments, their idiosyncrasies and eccentricities provide enough material for a gripping murder mystery. But what could have been a taut suspense story meanders aimlessly taking the readers along to an uninspiring end. If both the novels have fallen short of the readers' expectations, it may be because the novelist has set a high standard for herself in her other published works. It is easy to see that what Deshpande is best at is the portrayal of human relationships and the turmoils raging in the minds of her female protagonists who are unfairly treated by their parents, husbands and society in general. Deshpande is so acutely aware of the inequalites present in society that even her detective stories are replete with examples to prove the same.

The chief female characters in *Come Up and Be Dead*, the school principal, Kshama, and her housekeeper/cousin, Devayani, are spinsters. They are typical examples of women caught between the modern idea of freedom and the traditional need for a husband and home of their own. Kshama is an efficient administrator and possesses an ostensibly unruffled manner but her thoughts reveal the agitation and complexes within her. Devayani seems quite content with her role as a housekeeper but we find her musing now and then about the uselessness of her life, "But I was neither daughter nor wife nor mother now. What was I then? Nothing? In a sense, it was restful to be nothing. And yet there was this feeling too. . . . I might as well be dead."[15] This may be Deshpande's way of showing that even a person as well-read as Devayani who quotes frequently from Shakespeare and Dickens, is still the product of a culture which declares woman's experience as incomplete without marriage. Through the character of Jyoti Raman, a school teacher, Deshpande also hints at the sexual aggression of men tolerated silently by women. Mrs. Raman is somehow able to free herself from her husband by threatening to commit suicide but there are many others who are not so lucky.

The narrator Manju in *If I Die Today*, is quite different from the average Indian woman who views matrimony and motherhood as the ultimate happiness in life. She resents the fact that her children are a barrier to her independence. Motherhood, she thinks, "is a trap, keeping you in a cage until you lose the desire for freedom until you forget what the word 'freedom' means."[16] It is obvious also that she does not approve of her daughter displaying any typically female characteristics like fear or cowardice. She thinks: "I didn't want her to grow up a clinging vine. I wanted her to be fearless and independent." (45) Deshpande also tries to unmask the outwardly sophisticated and well-educated person's yearning for a son and heir. Pitying Mriga for being unkindly treated by her 'Oh-so-foreign' father, Dr. Kulkarni, Manju thinks: "Behind the pipe-smoking perfectly mannered phlegmatic style that he cultivated, was he after all, just a traditional Hindu man longing for a son and heir? And taking it out on poor Mriga because she was only a girl?" (36) Deshpande also lays bare the feeble male ego which cannot tolerate the idea of female superiority. Finding a sympathetic listener in Manju, Tony unburdens his marital problems to her:

> Don't let them tell you. It doesn't matter who earns more money in a marriage. It does. There was Cyn before marriage crazy about me, looking up to me, ready to do anything for me. It didn't matter at all that I was just a Games Master and she was a medico. We were just crazy about each other. (84)

Tony very succinctly sums up the main ingredient for a happy marriage. He is happy so long as his wife looks up to him but when she starts earning more than he does, he begins to think that she is patronising him. The same situation is dealt with in *The Dark Holds No Terrors* where it is the main theme of the novel. It is obvious that in both her detective novels too, Deshpande is unable to remain unconcerned about the inner turmoils and sense of unfairness experienced by her female protagonists.

The voice of Deshpande's female protagonists is even more pronounced in her short stories. Her collection of short stories, *The Legacy*, has had the distinction of being prescribed as a text book in Columbia university for a course in modern literature. The primary focus of attention in her short stories is woman—her frustrations, pain and anguish. Her stories revolve around middle-class women in India who are unable to defy social convention and seek a compromise as a way out of their dilemma. "An Antidote to Boredom" is the story of a woman dissatisfied with her existence as the wife of an indifferent man and finds herself involved with a young widower. Plagued with feelings of guilt towards her son (not husband) and nagged by the doubt whether she is merely seeking an antidote to boredom in her affair, she lets the opportunity go, bitterly regretting it later. According to G.S. Amur who has prefaced the book and considers this the best story in the collection, the story "dramatises the suffering of a woman who makes an unsuccessful attempt to escape from the prison of her fixed role as wife and live a life of spontaneity."[17]

"The Intrusion" records the horror of a newly married woman whose crass and insensitive husband violates her body exercising his conjugal rights. "A Liberated Woman" is the story of the catastrophic result of a marriage between a popular woman doctor and a mediocre college lecturer, because of the wounded male ego. Deshpande apparently felt that she could not do justice to the theme within the framework of a short story. Hence, she subsequently expanded the same idea in the form of her novel, *The Dark Holds No Terrors*. "Death of a Child" is the story of a lonely woman and her experience of guilt and shame caused by an abortion for which she is to be blamed. "Why a Robin" is a highly sensitive story of a mother who feels isolated from her only daughter who has more in common with her father. The situation changes dramatically, however, when the child clings to her mother for comfort and security, on attaining puberty, thus giving a new meaning to the mother's life.

"It Was Dark," the title story in the volume of short stories by the same name is a moving tale of the rape of school-girl. Deshpande evocatively brings out the despair and anguish of her parents, particularly of the mother, who feels crushed with the feeling of guilt for having never cautioned her daughter on the dangers that might befall her. In "The Inner Rooms," Deshpande recreates a passage from *The Mahabharata* making the readers empathise with the plight of Amba bringing a new dimension to the oft-told story. "A Wall is Safer" highlights the injustice meted out to a woman who is expected to sacrifice her career to safeguard her marriage. The protagonist, Hema, a professionally qualified and practising lawyer has no option but to throw up her career and follow her husband, Vasanth into wilderness, close to the project he has undertaken. Hema's friend and colleague Sushma is aghast and asks Vasanth what he expects Hema to do in the 'middle of nowhere.' Vasanth replies without hesitation that she can take up teaching. Sushma retorts that she is a lawyer and not a teacher and asks him if he would change his profession overnight. She makes a valid point here challenging most men's attitude towards their wives' careers.

The title story in the volume *It Was the Nightingale* is written in contrast to "A Wall is Safer." Here, the protagonist, lovingly called Jayu by her husband, is all set to go abroad for a couple of years to pursue her career. Though she is aware that the long separation will be equally painful for both herself and her husband, she is determined not to let the opportunity go. She justifies her decision by saying, "To me, our lives are intertwined, yet they are two different strands."[18] The protaganist in "A Man and a Woman" is a young passionate widow who develops an illicit physical relationship with her younger brother-in-law. "The Duel" is the story of a widow who succumbs to the seduction of a male writer. These stories are examples of Deshpande's bold assertion of woman's sexuality. In "A Day Like Another," the wife is aware of husband's infidelity but does not revolt, for the sake of domestic harmony. She would rather suffer the pain and humiliation than revolt and upset the relationship which has taken years to build.

The story, "I Want," in the volume, *The Miracle and Other Stories*, revolves around the protagonist whose opinions are never taken into account—first by her father with regard to her marriage, and later by her fiance with regard to her career. As a girl who has crossed the generally accepted marriageable age, she is expected to marry the first man who agrees to marry her. She is also expected to give in to his wishes and express no such desire which might jeopardise the proposal. Her opinions and aspirations therefore remain unvoiced. The husband in the story, "The Shadow," is broad-minded enough to accept his wife who has committed adultery, but his generosity does not stretch any further to accommodate the child born of this union. Perhaps this is expecting too much from men who normally do not tolerate even the slightest deviation from socially-accepted behaviour on the part of their wives. "The Awakening" is a pathetic story of a young girl's sudden awareness of the harsh realities of life. Deshpande very sensitively depicts the dreams and aspirations of a young girl on the threshold of life who is forced to come to a compromise and take on the responsiblities of her family on her young shoulders.

Most of the short stories are reprinted in a single paperback edition entitled *The Intrusion and Other Stories*, published by Penguin India in 1993. Almost all her short stories are women-centred, dealing with woman in different roles—wife, mother, daughter and an individual in a society conditioned by the rigid codes laid down by man. The short stories are therefore as true to life and representative of the dilemma faced by modern women, as her novels. As G.S. Amur rightly observes: "Woman's struggle, in the context of contemporary Indian society, to find and preserve her identity as wife, mother and most important of all, as human being is Shashi Deshpande's major concern as a creative writer, and this appears in all her important stories." (10)

A comprehensive analysis of all her work leaves one in no doubt about where Deshpande's sympathies lie. It would be unfair to label her 'feminist' and categorise her with several other writers who differ from her in varying degrees. She can at best be called an articulator of women who are caught at the crossroads of change in a society which is undergoing the birthpangs of transition from tradition to modernity. It is a difficult job, indeed, to give voice to women who themselves are not sure of their own suffering and who stand in an unenviable position today. They are acutely aware of the injustices heaped on them but are condemned to live the life of suppression which was the lot of their predecessors. In many ways, their condition is even more pitiable than that of women of earlier generations who unquestioningly accepted their secondary position in society. Her novels contain so much that is the material of feminist thought—myriad roles of woman as mother/wife/daughter, identity crisis and women's sexuality—that all those who have interviewed her so far have inevitably asked her as to what extent she considers herself a feminist. She says:

> I now have no doubts at all in saying that I am a feminist. In my own life, I mean. But not consciously, as a novelist. I must also say that my feminism has come to me very slowly, very gradually, and mainly out of my own thinking and experiences and feelings. I started writing first and only then discovered my feminism. And it was much later that I actually read books about it.[19]

Perhaps, the reason why Deshpande takes exception to her works being labelled 'feminist' is the misconception in the minds of most people regarding the term, feminism.

Other women writers have voiced similar apprehensions and it is interesting to observe their reactions to being thus classified. In an interview conducted by Sue Dickman, many important women writers in English and the regional languages in India have, not surprisingly, expressed similar sentiments. Mahasweta Devi, the well-known Bengali writer and Sahitya Akademi Award winner, who is also a social activist, says:

> I am a woman, and I am writing. But I am not writing of women alone. What I am writing, most of my books, it is about class exploitation, the under class is exploited, men, women together. Of course, women get the worst part of it, but not always.[20]

Mahasweta Devi, like Mulk Raj Anand, is more concerned with exploitation than gender exploitation, but she admits that women are at a greater disadvantage among the exploited lower classes. C.S. Lakshmi (Ambai), a Tamil writer, who also has a few film scripts to her credit, has reservations about being called a woman writer. She says: "When a man writes, even when he writes about a woman, it has universal qualities. But when I write, if it is about a woman, it gets particularised."[21]

Deshpande is equally uncomfortable about being categorised as a woman-writer and denies being a feminist writer with a mission. She does not trace the influence in her writing of the feminists like Simone de Beauvoir or Germaine Greer, though she agrees that they helped to place her confusions, and put them in order. She, however, maintains that she read the works of these feminists much after she started writing. The issues which she feels strongly about are the degradation that women experience and continue to experience and the subordination and inequality. According to her:

> Feminism is not a matter of theory. It is difficult to apply Kate Millett or Simone de Beauvoir or whoever to the reality of our daily lives in India. And then there are such terrible misconceptions about feminism by people here. They often think it is about burning bras and walking out on your husband, children or about not being married, not having children etc. I always try to make the point now about what feminism is not, and to say that we have to discover what it is in our own lives, our experiences. And I actually feel that a lot of women in India are feminists without realising it.[22]

Deshpande feels that women have a tremendous inner strength, but so much of that strength is used up in merely enduring. Her idea of feminism is best summed up in her words: "for me feminism is translating what is used up in endurance into something positive: a real strength."

NOTES

1. Sushila Singh, "Preface," *Feminism and Recent Fiction in English* (New Delhi: Prestige, 1991), 7.
2. Quoted in *Hunter College Women's Studies Collective: Women's Realities, Women's Choices: Introduction to Women's Studies* (New Delhi: Oxford University Press, 1983), 68.

3. Linda Gordon, quoted in the "Preface," *Feminism and Recent Fiction in English*, 8.
4. Simone de Beauvoir, "Introduction," *The Second Sex*, trans. and ed. H.M. Parshley (1953; rpt. Harmondsworth: Penguin, 1983), 13.
5. Betty Freidan, *The Feminine Mystique* (1963; rpt. Harmondsworth: Penguin, 1971), 282.
6. Quoted in Kate Millett, *Sexual Politics* (1969; rpt. London: Rupert Hart Davis, 1971), 56-57.
7. Germaine Greer, *The Female Eunuch* (1970; rpt. St. Alabama: Paladin, 1976), 319.
8. Sylvia Plath, *The Bell Jar* (1963; rpt. London: Faber & Faber, 1982), 88-89.
9. Anne Stevenson, "Writing as a Woman," *Women Writing and Writing about Women*, ed. Mary Jacobus (USA: Harper & Row, 1979).
10. Shanta Krishnaswamy, "Raja Rao: The Doomed Pattern of Saved Males and Doomed Females," *Glimpses of Women in India* (New Delhi: Ashish, 1983).
11. Shashi Deshpande, "The Dilemma of a Woman Writer," *The Literary Criterion*, Vol. 20, No. 4, 1985, 33.
12. Henrik Ibsen quoted by Inga-Steva Ewebank, "Ibsen and the Language of Women," *Women Writing and Writing about Women.*
13. P. Ramamoorthy, "My Life is My Own: A Study of Shashi Deshpande's Women," *Feminism and Recent Fiction in English*, 115.
14. Shashi Deshpande, "Of Concerns, Of Anxieties," *Indian Literature*, Vol. XXXIX, No. 5, Sept.-Oct. 1996, 107.
15. Shashi Deshpande, *Come Up and Be Dead* (New Delhi: Vikas, 1983), 119.
16. Shashi Deshpande, *If I Die Today* (New Delhi: Vikas, 1983), 47.
17. G.S. Amur, "Preface," *The Legacy and Other Stories* (Calcutta: Writer's Workshop, 1978), 10.
18. Shashi Deshpande, *It Was the Nightingale* (Calcutta: Writer's Workshop, 1986), 13.
19. Lakshmi Holmstrom, Interview, "Shashi Deshpande Talks to Lakshmi Holmstrom," *Wasafiri*, No. 17, Spring, 1983, 26.
20. Sue Dickman, "In Conversation: Sue Dickman with Indian Women Writers," *The Book Review*, Vol. 19, No. 4, Apr. 1995, 33.
21. Lakshmi Holmstrom, *Wasafiri*, 26.
22. *Ibid.*, 26.

"A Restricting Bond": *Roots and Shadows*

> Man has regarded woman as his tool. She has learnt to be his tool, and in the end found this easy and comfortable to be such, because when one drags another in his fall the descent is easy.
>
> Mahatma Gandhi, *Harijan*

Shashi Deshpande's first full-length novel, *Roots and Shadows*, features an educated, middle-class woman protagonist, Indu, who, like her counterparts in Deshpande's other novels, *That Long Silence* and *The Dark Holds No Terrors*, finds herself suffocating under the stranglehold of our tradition-bound society.

The novel deals with Indu's attempt to assert herself as an individual. This process brings her into confrontation with her family and society in general. The novel begins with the marriage of Mini, Indu's cousin, which is performed in a traditional way in their ancestral home. It makes Indu think retrospectively about the events which led to her returning home after a gap of eleven years. The eighteen-year-old rebel, who leaves home to live life her own way, returns on being summoned by the old matriarch, *Akka*, who is on her death bed. Indu is drawn once more into the vortex of the family as *Akka* makes her the sole beneficiary of all her property. From here the spotlight shifts to all the myriad characters in the novel. Deshpande brings alive a large Maharashtrian Brahmin household with her characteristic eye for detail. She successfully portrays the baser human emotions like greed and jealousy which are bound to be present in an atmosphere charged with resentment by the family at being excluded from the will. The novel, however, stands out particularly for the stark presentation of its women characters—their hopes, their fears, their disappointments and their anguish.

In the long list of women characters in the novel, the portrayal of the tyrannical and matriarchal figure, *Akka*, deserves special mention. She is a rich childless widow who opts to stay in her brother's house after the death of her husband. That she wields tremendous influence in the house is obvious from the beginning. Since the day she enters the house she maintains absolute control over her brother's children. Indu graphically narrates how "*Kaka* even after becoming a grandfather, could be reduced to a red-faced, stuttering school boy by *Akka*'s venomous tongue."[1]

Akka represents the old order, fanatically obsessed with keeping caste, so much so that even when she is on her death bed she refuses to move into a hospital because as she puts it, "God knows what caste the nurses are or the doctors. I could not drink a drop of water there." (24) *Akka* is also very particular about how a girl should talk, dress or behave. She reprimands Indu severely for daring to talk to a boy in the lone corner of a library. It is a known fact in the house that she had put her foot down when Naren's mother wanted to learn music, saying:

> What, learn music from a strange man! Sit and sing in front of strangers! Like THOSE women? Are we that kind of family? Isn't it enough for you to sing one or two devotional songs, one or two aarti songs? What more does a girl from a decent family need to know? (55)

Akka herself is a victim of gender oppression but she perpetuates the same victimization as far as her influence extends. Indu who grows up with no fond feelings towards *Akka*, learns her story through Narmada *Atya*, only after her death. Narmada *Atya*'s narration immediately evokes the reader's pity and focusses attention on the plight of all those victims of child marriage who were sometimes forced to undergo inhuman treatment, bound as they were by the shackles of marriage. Indu often recollects *Akka*'s story in Narmada *Atya*'s words:

> She was just 12 when she was married. And he was well past 30. Remember him still. He was a tall, bulky man with large, coarse features. And she . . . she was small, dainty, really pretty, with her round face, fair skin, straight nose and curly hair. Six months after her marriage, she 'grew up' and went to her husband's home. What she had to endure there, no one knows. She never told anyone. Our grandfather, her father, was a man who kept himself aloof. No one could approach him easily. And her mother, our grandmother, died when she was a child. But I heard that twice she tried to run away—a girl of 13. Her mother-in-law, I heard, whipped her for that and locked her up for three days, starved her as well. And then, sent her back to her husband's room. The child, they said, cried and clung to her mother-in-law saying, "Lock me up again, lock me up." But there was no escape from a husband then. I remember her telling me before my own marriage was consummated, "Now your punishment begins, Narmada. You have to pay for all those saris and jewels." (77)

Sex as punishment was, perhaps, how it was viewed by such child brides who nevertheless did not raise any banner of revolt but on the other hand continued to suffer and helped to perpetuate such oppression. As Tara Ali Baig comments, "Arch traditionalists that women are, it is they who have successfully and brutally established man's ascendency over woman in society."[2] Through the character of *Akka*, Deshpande successfully portrays the contradictory traits in a woman's character. That *Akka* was a domineering character is evident from Narmada's narration where she tells Indu about the way she controls her husband after he suffers from a stroke which leaves him totally paralyzed. He lives for two years in this condition when *Akka* takes care of him excellently, displaying her sati-dharma. But she gets back at him for all that she had endured earlier by not allowing his mistress, whom he adores, to meet him. She even takes a vicious pleasure in informing him that she threw his mistress out when she had come to meet him. Narmada, who is just a child then, is moved to tears by the grief experienced by *Akka*'s husband on hearing this from his wife. Later that night Narmada also finds *Akka* in tears and learns from her that no night passed when she did not cry after getting married.

Through the portrayal of *Akka*'s marriage, Deshpande makes a strong statement on the so-called arranged marriages which are so unfair to women. A husband who finds his wife incompatible has at least the option of finding for himself another woman to satisfy his need; but a wife in a similar situation has no option but to lead a loveless life. Narmada's narration also highlights the tragedy of the mistress who had given *Akka*'s husband the best years of her life, but is now doomed to face humiliation. As Neena Arora remarks: "Man considers it as normal behaviour to satisfy his desires at both the emotional and the physical levels outside marriage, while it is ruthlessly condemned as adultery in case a woman indulges in it even though accidentally the slightest hint of any deviation on her part which may not even involve sex, man turns violent and hostile towards his wife and starts prosecuting her. This condemnation is dictated by man's interest in preserving his property rather than by any moral consideration."[3]

When *Akka* returns to her father's house after the death of her husband she enforces a rigid code of conduct on women under her influence like Indu, by insisting that a woman should never utter her husband's name as it would shorten his life span and that it showed disrespect. Indu reacts vehemently to such talk and exclaims, "what connection can there be between a man's longevity and his wife's calling him by name? It's as bad as praying to the *Tulsi* to increase his life span." (35) Indu as an educated, upper middle-class woman resents such traditional practices but like the protagonists of Deshpande's other novels, Jaya and Saru, she is caught in the web woven by age-old custom and tradition. Though her education and exposure encourage her to break free from the clutches of tradition, she eventually finds that she is no different from the women who circumambulate the *Tulsi* plant and who believe that a woman's good fortune lies in dying before her husband. She draws this conclusion about herself from the fact that she loves her husband enough to want him by her side all the time, forever. Her husband, Jayant, in spite of his seemingly western style of living, is no different from the average Indian male. He expects his wife to be passive and submissive. Any display of passion or desire on her behalf shocks him.

There are several instances in the novel which subtly prove that Indu has always been playing the role of a perfect wife in order to keep her husband happy and satisfied. The most glaring example is Jayant's insistence that she should continue working for her magazine even when he knows how frustrating it is for her. Indu narrates the story of how she once interviewed a social worker who received an award for her services. Indu was suitably impressed by the woman who was "soft-spoken, articulate, seemingly sincere and dedicated." (18) After writing up the article, Indu was given another article written about the same woman by an old man. Indu was shocked to read it. She thought: "This . . . was a story of shameless exploitation of ignorance, poverty and need. A story of ruthlessness and unscrupulousness in the pursuit of fame, power and money, all of which had come now." (18) She went to her editor with both the copies and, worldly-wise as he was, he refused to accept the copy written by the old man, though he admitted that it was true. Indu was taken aback by the hypocrisy of the woman and the attitude of the editor. She narrated the story to Jayant and expected him to stand by what was right, but contrary to her expectations he replied, "That's life! What can one person do against the whole system! No point making yourself ridiculous with futile gestures. We need the money, don't we? Don't forget we have a long way to go." (19)

Indu therefore continues working, albeit hating every moment of it. She stifles her conscience and writes only that which will be accepted by the editor and the public. It also disturbs her to realize that she has left her middle-class values behind to become a part of the success-oriented society. She is overcome by a sense of futility. She, perhaps, would have continued to live this way if she was not summoned by *Akka* and if she did not meet

Naren. Her reunion with Naren offers her an opportunity to vent her frustrations and review her life objectively. She relates to Naren her life with Jayant in detail:

> We belong to the smart young set. Do you know what that means? Fresh flowers in the house everyday. Can you believe it, Naren. I've gone and done a course in flower arrangement? The best places, whether you go out to eat or to cut your hair. Freshly laundered clothes twice a day. Clothes . . . yes, we have to keep up with the latest trends . . . we don't have friends, but the right contacts and "people one should know." Who entertain us just as often as we entertain them. And when we get together . . . oh, you should listen to us Naren. We talk with nostalgia of places abroad. We're gay and whimsical about our own people . . . our own country. We are rational, unprejudiced, broad-minded. We discuss intelligently, even solemnly, the problems of unemployment, poverty, corruption and family planning. We scorn the corrupt. We despise the ignorant, we hate the wicked—and our hearts bleed, Naren for Vietnam, for the blacks, for the Harijans—but frankly we don't care a damn not one goddamn about anything but our own precious selves, our own precious walled in lives. (28)

This emotional outburst from Indu proves that she had been exercising extreme control over herself in order to protect her marriage. It is difficult for her to accept her compromise in this matter as she had all along fooled herself that she was different from her *Kakis* and *Atyas*. As P. Bhatnagar comments: "It baffled her to realize that she who had considered herself to be so independent, so intelligent, so clever; she who had been so proud of her logical and rational thinking; she who had been all set to reform Indian womanhood had fallen into the trap waiting for her."[4]

Throughout the novel, there are several examples which prove that Indu is very conscious of the unfairness prevailing in society with regard to women. There are so many small incidents in everyday life which we simply take for granted but Indu highlights these incidents and makes us look anew at them and wonder at the injustice. Men are not even aware of the drudgery and the disgust involved in the countless household chores performed regularly by women. One such scene is graphically described by Indu:

> I went into the house avoiding the hall, ugly now with all the aftermath of an eaten meal. It disgusted me to see the strewn plates, the scattered remnants. And yet, for a whole lifetime, women patiently cleared up the mess with their bare hands after each meal. And women like ***Kaki*** even ate off the same dirty plate their husbands had eaten in earlier. Martyrs, heroines, or just stupid fools. (73)

Domestic chores as Indu describes, can be terribly tiresome, boring and frustrating. This is also observed by Simone de Beauvoir who says: "Few tasks are more like the torture of Sisyphus than housework, with its endless repetition; the clean becomes soiled, the soiled is made clean, over and over, day after day. The housewife wears herself out marking time. She makes nothing, simply perpetuates the present."[5]

There are several other examples to show how sharply aware Indu is of the prevailing injustice in society. If most people are unaware of this injustice, it only proves that they have been nurtured since childhood in a society which perpetuates such inequalities. In the early formative years of the child, which are critical for later personality development, he or she is exposed to traditional patterns, which sharply define the male/female pattern of behaviour. It is indoctrined in the girl-child to play the role of a disciplined daughter, a meek and submissive wife and daughter-in-law, and a sacrificing mother. The exaggerated importance given to the virginity of a girl is also greatly responsible for enforcing a restriction on her movements as soon as she reaches puberty. Any girl who tries to rebel against such rules is severely reprimanded and shown her place. In one of her conversations with Naren, Indu tries to explain herself to him:

> How will you understand, Naren, you who have never had to fight, to turn aggressive, to assert yourself? How easily it comes to you, just because you are a man, for me—as a child they had told me I must be obedient and unquestioning. As a girl they had told me I must be meek and submissive. Why? I had asked. Because you are a female. You must accept everything, even defeat with grace because you are a girl, they said. It is the only way, they said, for a female to live and survive. (174)

Indu also bitterly recollects how crudely the idea of her womanhood was thrust upon her. Naren's question as to why she always fought for her womanhood makes her think in retrospection about the day when she was first made aware of it:

> My womanhood. . . . I had never thought of it until the knowledge had been thrust brutally, gracelessly on me the day, I had grown up "You're a woman now," Kaki had told me. "You can have babies yourself?" I, a woman? My mind had flung off the thought with an amazing swiftness. I was only a child. And then, she had gone on to tell me badly, crudely, how I could have a baby. And I who had all the child's unselfconsciousness about my own body, had, for the first time, felt an immense hatred for it. "And don't forget," she had ended, "for four days now you are unclean. You can't touch anyone or anything." And that had been my introduction to the beautiful world of being a woman. I was unclean. (87)

Simone de Beauvoir expresses something similar when she talks of "the dramatic conflict that harrows the adolescent girl at puberty: she cannot become 'grown-up' without accepting her femininity; and she knows already that her sex condemns her to a mutilated and fixed existence, which she faces at this time under the form of impure sickness and a vague sense of guilt." (351)

Right from her childhood, Indu also observes the secondary

position occupied by women in the family. It is unthinkable for a woman to have a cup of tea sent to her room. Indu lightheartedly mocks the women's reaction if she were to do something as brazen as that. She laughingly asks her *Kaka*, "Can you imagine them sending up a cup of tea for me? Women and children should know their places." (53) The shaven head of a widow, a domestic help, reminds Indu of the plight of all widows—those who shaved their heads to avoid censure and those who didn't and are treated like out-castes. Looking at the widow's shaven head, Indu says:

> The bare skull, with its short hairs, looked somehow not only indecent, but obscene when bared. And I understood why *Kaka* had, when *Atya* was widowed, so stoutly resisted the idea of her becoming a shaven widow. He had won but at the cost of *Atya*'s status. She was now a second class citizen in the kingdom of widows. The orthodox would not eat food cooked by her. (130)

Indu is also made deeply aware of her shortcomings as a complete woman in the eyes of all those conventional women who had their own standards for judging people. In the eyes of such a woman, she says:

> Nothing about me—my academic distinctions, my career my success, my money—none of these would impress her. To her I was just a childless woman. To get married, to bear children, to have sons and then grandchildren they were still for them the only success a woman could have. I had almost forgotten this breed of women since I had left home. (128)

However, in spite of her obvious feminist stance, in spite of her being highly sensitive to the injustice shown to women, and in spite of being educated and economically independent, Indu realizes that she is no different from the women like her *Atyas* and *Kakis*. From her outburst to Naren it is obvious that she is disillusioned by her husband Jayant's materialistic attitude to life. Her husband also resents any display of passion on her part. He expects his wife to be demure and coy, without shedding her inhibitions even in the privacy of their bedroom. This is evident from what Indu narrates, "Jayant, so passionate, so ready, sitting up suddenly and saying, 'no, not now,' when I had taken the initiative." (91) Her intimate tete-a-tete with Naren also reveals the pain and humiliation she experiences at being rebuffed in this manner. In a voice choked with emotion, she confides to Naren: "And now I know . . . it shocks him to find passion in a woman. It puts him off. When I'm like that, he turns away from me. I've learnt my lesson now. And so I pretend. I'm passive. And unresponsive. I'm still and dead." (92)

It is difficult for Indu, however, to remain totally indifferent to her husband. Her home-coming after a long exile makes her feel tremendously happy but, for her, this happiness is incomplete without Jayant by her side. She thinks, "This is my real sorrow. That I can never be complete in myself." (34) Her hard-won independence seems only an ephemera when she honestly questions herself if she is indeed independent. Under the guise of independence, the rebel in her had conditioned herself to become as submissive as any other Indian wife. Looking back in retrospection, she realizes that it is Jayant's wants that had always mattered to her: "When I look into the mirror, I think of Jayant, when I undress I think of him. Have I become a fluid with no shape, no form of my own?" (54) It frightens her that she was on the way to becoming an "ideal woman. A woman who sheds her 'I,' who loses her identity in her husband's." (54)

This desperate need to assert herself combined with the attraction she felt for her cousin, Naren, and the easy compatibility between them makes her take a daring step in surrendering herself to him. It is to be observed that she refuses to be consumed by guilt after committing adultery. She in fact revels in the act with wild abandon and deliberately savours the memory of it, refusing to wipe it out of her mind. She thinks:

I can go back and lie on my bed, I thought, and it will be

> like erasing the intervening period and what happened between Naren and me. But deliberately I went to my bed and began folding the covers. I don't need to erase anything I have done, I told myself in a fit of bravado. (168)

She feels that her sexual encounter with Naren has nothing to do with Jayant, and so she resolves not to tell him anything about it. This bold assertion of her self has sparked off contradictory remarks from the reviewers. Commenting on her decision not to reveal this to her husband, P. Ramamoorthy says: "This sheds a brilliant light on Indu's awareness of her autonomy and her realization that she is a being, and not a dependent on Jayant. The novel gains its feminist stance in Indu's exploration into herself but it also moves beyond the boundaries of feminism into a perception of the very predicament of the human existence."[6]

This same incident is, however, seen in a totally different light by P. Bhatnagar who laments the fact that she had to commit adultery to come to terms with her married life. She feels that, "Indu's casual and matter-of fact attitude to what she had done is shocking. Have our morals really gone so low that women commit this sin for nothing, just to prove that they do not lack courage? Is this really representative of the modern Indian woman?" (129)

Perhaps this is Deshpande's answer to the double standards practised by our society where only men are allowed to take sexual liberties. Deshpande, in the *Roots and Shadows*, also highlights the problem faced by middle-class people in finding suitable grooms for their daughters. This is aptly illustrated in the case of Padmini. After an interminable search when a boy finally agrees to marry her, the marriage is settled without further hesitation. This in spite of the fact that the boy had "heavy, coarse features and crude mannerisms." (3) Padmini's acceptance of this marriage makes Indu wonder, "A woman's life, they had told me, contained no choices. And all my life, specially in this house, I had seen the truth of this. The women had no choice but to submit, to accept. And I had often wondered . . . have they been born without wills, or have their wills atrophied through a lifetime of disuse? And yet Mini, who had no choice either, had accepted the reality, the finality, with a grace and composure that spoke eloquently of that inner strength." (6)

Mini's stoic acceptance of her partner in marriage reminds the reader of Charlotte, in Jane Austen's celebrated *Pride and Prejudice*. Charlotte unhesitatingly agrees to marry the ridiculous Collins for the fear of remaining unmarried if she let the opportunity slip by. It is indeed a tragedy that almost two hundred years later Indian girls echo the same sentiment where "it was marriage that mattered, not the man." (4) In reply to Indu's persistent questions about the reasons for her accepting to marry someone who obviously is no match for her, Mini tells Indu that she is marrying him because there is nothing else she can do except look after a home and to have a home she needs to marry. On probing further, Indu elicits a reply from Mini who aptly sums up the trauma faced by most Indian girls on the threshold of marriage:

> You don't know what it has been like. Watching *Kaka* and Hemant and even Madhav *Kaka* running around after eligible men. And then sending the horoscope and having it come back with a message, it doesn't match? And if the horoscope matched there was the meeting to be arranged. And mother and *Atya* slogging in the kitchen the whole day. And all those people coming and staring and asking all kinds of questions. And if we heard they were old fashioned people, I would dress up in an old fashioned manner and they would say, 'She's not modern enough.' And if I dressed up well, they would say, "She's too fashionable for us. Or too short. Or too tall. Or too something." And *Kaka* trying to laugh and talk to those people, while his eyes looked so . . . anxious. And I, feeling like as if I had committed a great crime by being born a girl. So we would have to go through with it all over again. And finally if everything was fine, there was the dowry. (135)

Through the example of Mini, Deshpande raises the issue of arranged marriage—the obvious absence of sentiment or feeling in a union which sanctified the lifelong partnership of man and woman. Indu is moved enough to comment: "Behind the facade of romanticism, sentiment and tradition, what was marriage after all, but two people brought together after cold-blooded bargaining to meet, mate and reproduce so that the generations might continue?" (3)

It is to be observed, however, that Deshpande desists from making hysterical anti-dowry statements and instead tries to look at the problem without any preconceived ideas. She lays bare the hypocrisy and double standards practised by society. Padmini's mother and other relations do not consider the easily available Naren a suitable match for their daughter. They would rather pay a hefty dowry and settle for someone who has little to recommend him other than his family's position in society. "They would," argues Indu, think of everything, "the families. the communities, the stars, the *gotras*," and leave out "that great incalculable."

Towards the end of the novel, Indu eventually meets up to her own expectations of an emancipated woman by the way she puts *Akka*'s wealth to use—spending it on Mini's wedding and Vithal's education. She takes this decision at the risk of offending her numerous relatives each of whom has his or her own idea of how the money should be spent. The list includes the dead Naren who had vehemently opposed the idea of Vithal being educated with *Akka*'s money, and *Akka* herself who would never have wanted her money to be spent on anyone outside the family. But Indu, after serious introspection decides to act according to her wish without taking into consideration the likes and dislikes of the living and the dead alike. She refuses to take heed of the promise she had made to Naren, telling herself that it is the living who need our loyalty, not the dead.

Towards the end, Indu does achieve her freedom, refusing to let herself be influenced by *Kaka*, *Atya* or even Jayant, in doing what she believes is the right thing to do. She who had earlier been cowed down by Jayant's disapproval of her giving up her job now gathers enough courage to stand by her decision.

Jayant who is initially bewildered by her attitude, finally acknowledges her right to make her own decisions and recognises her strength which she has never displayed earlier. He even comforts Indu who despairs of not finding a publisher for her book by saying, "I will publish it for you." (15) For Indu, this assurance by her husband is the ultimate in happiness.

Indu's dilemma is representative of the larger predicament faced by women in modern India where a slow transition threatens to shake the age-old social set-up to its very roots. The most obvious symbol of change is the break up of the joint family. The total contrast in the life style of the joint family in which Indu was reared, and her own home which consisted of only her husband and herself, is evident. The breaking up of the joint family has affected relationships at various levels but most glaringly the relationship between spouses. In a joint family, "husbands and wives . . . their worlds touched briefly in the darkness of the night," (46) as Indu puts it. This brief meeting gave them little occasion for conflict. In the nuclear family pattern, however, husband and wife are constantly thrown together, placing a greater responsibility on both, giving rise to situations which may lead to incompatibility, frustration and disappointment in each other. The wife especially is more vulnerable, with her new-found desire for freedom and the age-old tradition of male dominance.

Shashi Deshpande suggests through the character of Indu that there is a greater chance of happiness for women if they learn to conquer their fears and assert themselves. As P. Bhatnagar comments, "Thus Shashi Deshpande makes her heroine choose security through reconciliation. The ethos in the novel is neither of victory nor of defeat but of harmony and understanding between two opposing ideas and conflicting selves. This is quite representative of the basic Indian attitude." (128)

The novel ends on a note of hope with the protagonist, Indu, asserting herself as an individual and putting an end to her doubts about herself. That she is able to hold her own in a household full of tradition-bound men and women is proof of her individuality. In breaking traditional ground, she is also careful to delineate her presence on yet another dimension—as one who is qualified to defy the status quo with not only courage but also with the conviction of rationale and accountability. In a global drama involving the dance of the sexes, she emerges as an intelligent, attractive and wholly practical woman who is not lured into a relationship but enters into it fully aware of the consequences and confident that she is not stretching her moral obligations.

NOTES

1. Shashi Deshpande, *Roots and Shadows: A Novel* (Madras: Sangam Books, 1983), 24.
2. Quoted in Meera Shirwadkar, *Image of Woman in the Indo-Anglian Novel* (New Delhi: Sterling, 1979), 26.
3. Neena Arora, *Nayantara Sahgal and Doris Lessing—A Feminist Study in Comparison* (New Delhi: Prestige, 1991), 61.
4. P. Bhatnagar, "Indian Womanhood: Fight for Freedom in *Roots and Shadows*," *Indian Women Novelists*, ed. R.K. Dhawan (New Delhi: Prestige, 1991), Set I, Vol. V, 121.
5. Simone de Beauvoir, *The Second Sex*, trans. and ed. H.M. Parshley (1953; rpt. Harmondsworth: Penguin, 1983), 470.
6. P. Ramamoorthy, "My Life is My Own: A Study of Shashi Deshpande's Women," *Feminism and Recent Fiction in English*, ed. Sushila Singh (New Delhi: Prestige, 1991), 124.

"You are your own refuge": *The Dark Holds No Terrors*

> I looked and it was a revelation: this world was a masculine world, my childhood had been nourished by myths forged by men and I hadn't reacted to them in at all the same way I should have done if I had been a boy.
>
> Simone de Beauvoir, *Force of Circumstance*

> You are your own refuge. There is no other refuge. This refuge is hard to achieve.
>
> *Dhammapada*

Shashi Deshpande's second novel, *The Dark Holds No Terrors* is about a well-educated, economically independent woman's search for her identity which leads to uncover the dormant strength in human beings. It is the story of Sarita (called Saru) and her relationship with her parents and her husband and her agonizing search for herself. It is the story of a marriage on the verge of breakdown and of a woman who has been made acutely conscious of her gender since childhood.

The novel opens with Saru returning to her parents' house after a gap of fifteen years. She had walked out once, with a vow never to return. Nevertheless, she returns to seek refuge, unable to bear the barbarism of her husband. Her stay in her parents' house gives her a chance to review her relationship with her husband, her mother, her children, and her dead brother, Dhruva. The novel derives its strength, however, from the stark presentation of Saru's childhood, her trauma of being an unloved child and the equally stark presentation of her marriage to a man who is consumed by an inferiority complex which manifests itself in the form of sexual sadism.

The narrative vacillates between the present and the past, between the first person and the third, to focus on certain events in the past which have been too deeply etched in the mind of the protagonist to be erased and which, perhaps, have moulded and shaped her personality. Her earliest memories are those which underlined the discrimination shown by her mother in favour of her brother. His birthdays and other religious rituals related to him are given top priority and celebrated with much pomp and fanfare, whereas her birthdays are barely acknowledged. Saru often wonders if her birth was a cause of displeasure to her mother, as she later recalls:

> Birthdays were not then the tremendous occasions they are made out to be now; but the excitement of having one, of being the centre of attraction never palled. It was always a fascinating thought—'I was born.' But of my birth, my mother had said to me once. . . . "It rained heavily the day you were born. It was terrible." And somehow, it seemed to me that it was my birth that was terrible for her, not the rains.[1]

Saru recollects how on her brother Dhruva's birthdays, there was always a Puja held in the evenings. Going further back in memory, she remembers the sense of joyous excitement which pervaded their house on the occasion of his naming ceremony. Many such scenes are etched in her mind and the Indian view of the girl as a liability and the boy an asset are firmly implanted in her mind. Ragini Ramachandra however. feels that this aspect of the story does not ring true. She writes: "The portrayal of Sarita's mother who adored the son and neglected the daughter seems to be a weak point in the story. While one could accept a mother's preferences amongst her children, it seems rather incredible that she should live and die with curses on her lips for her female child, especially in the Indian context. The mother's monstrosity seems to serve as a rallying point for the novelist to bring her feminist ideas together. Hence the nagging feeling that the book has an axe to grind."[2] A careful reading of the novel would enable one to refute the charge. The preference for boys is blatantly acknowledged in most Indian homes. The reasons for such preferences are not difficult to understand. They are inextricably linked to the Indian psyche. It would be too simplistic to say that boys are preferred over girls because of the dowry they bring in at the time of marriage. The reasons are rooted in our tradition-bound society which demands the mandatory presence of the male child in important rituals. Our patriarchal society also considers only the male offspring as worthy enough to carry on the family line. As Sarabjit Sandhu observes: "The mother is very attached to her son. Her attitude is a typical one, after all, he is a male child and, therefore, one who will propagate the family lineage. In another sense, also, the male child is considered more important than a girl, because he is qualified to give 'agni' to his dead parents. The soul of the dead person would otherwise wander in ferment."[3]

The protagonist, Saru, had also to put up with constant reminders from her mother that she was dark complexioned and should not step into the sun lest it should worsen her colour. In one of her recapitulations, Saru records her conversation with her mother:

> "Don't go out in the sun, you'll get darker."
> "Who cares?"
> "We have to care if you don't. We have to get you married."
> "I don't want to get married."
> "Will you live with us all your life?"
> "Why not?"
> "You can't."
> "And Dhruva?"
> "He's different. He's a boy." (40)

This statement is firmly implanted in Saru's mind paving way for her rebellious attitude in future. In this connection, Saru's mother's attitude is typical of most Indian mothers and a common enough phenomenon in the Indian context.

Saru's problem is compounded when her brother accidentally dies by drowning. This becomes a turning point in her life. Her childhood memories are replete with her mother accusing her: "You did it, you did this, you killed him." (173) Saru's most important and recurrent childhood memory is that of her brother Dhruva's drowning in a pond. She is persistently haunted by the thought that she is responsible for his death because she is a mute spectator to the incident. When her mother accuses her of murdering her brother, she does not deny or refute the charge, because as Premila Paul observes, "When the mother accuses her of murder, she speaks out Saru's intentions and not the deed. Dhruva's demise had always been her subconscious desire and there is a very thin demarcation between her wish and its fulfilment."[4] This clearly indicates the height of sibling jealousy provoked, no doubt, by the mother's blatant favouritism. So strong is the mother's attachment to the son who would light her funeral pyre, that many years later, on hearing about her mother's death, Saru's immediate thought is, "Who lit the pyre? She had no son to do that for her. Dhruva had been seven when he died." (17)

Saru's mother's obvious preference for her brother, Dhruva, creates a sense of alienation within her and precipitates a sense of rootlessness and insecurity. Things become infinitely worse after Dhruva's death when her mother with her characteristic insensitivity blames her for his death. This obvious form of gender discrimination has been ignored by most writers whose stories are replete with loving and sacrificing mothers, irrespective of the child's gender. Mrinal Pande, the noted Hindi writer, presents this side of the story to some extent in her first work in English titled *Daughter's Daughter*, published quite appropriately in the International Year of the Girl Child. It is a loosely woven single narrative starting from when the author/narrator Tinu is about two, and proceeds to document her life through adolescence. There are several incidents mainly related to her annual trips to her maternal grandmother's home, where she realizes what it is to be the daughter's daughter, in contrast to the son's offspring.

She also describes the great rejoicing at the birth of her brother unlike the occasion of the arrival of her sister. These experiences are not restricted to any particular caste, region or period but span the experience of any Indian girl irrespective of geographical or chronological space.

However, this gender sensitivity can be observed in all the novels of Shashi Deshpande, especially in *The Dark Holds No Terrors*. It is surprising that gender discrimination viewed at this angle is not acknowledged by many Indian writers. But the fact remains that it is a significant factor in the Indian social set up. According to the research conducted by S. Anandalakshmi, Director, Lady Irwin College, Delhi:

> The supremacy of the male is so well established that the average Indian is surprised to even be queried about it. Whatever the ecology of the social group, even in communities where the women may be the breadwinners, the male is considered superior. Within the family the sense of inferiority of the female is pervasive. The sex ratio is unfavourable for girls and forces us to conclude that the survival of the girl is a matter of indifference in a considerable number of families. The birth of a son gives a woman status and she invests herself in her son's fixture, creating a deep symbiotic bond.[6]

It is no wonder then, that Saru's mother is left with no interest in living after her son's death. Her constant pining for her dead son and rejection of her daughter cause deep and indelible scars in Saru's mind. Her mother takes no particular interest in her education and personal advancement and snubs her at every given opportunity. This sense of rejection by her mother fills the mind of the adolescent Saru with a feeling of hatred towards her mother. The feeling is so intense that on attaining puberty she resentfully thinks, "If you are a woman, I don't want to be one," (62) detesting the fact that her body functioned in a similar manner as that of her mother's. Saru is also filled with a sense of shame at her monthly ordeal, praying desperately for a miracle to put an end to it. She resents the traditional practice in her orthodox home where she is treated like a pariah during those three days when she is made to sleep on a straw mat with a special cup and plate by her side in which she is served from a distance as her touch would mean pollution.

Without the support and understanding of a sympathetic mother, Saru develops an aversion to traditional practices in the crucial years of puberty and adolescence. The rejection by the mother during these impressionable years leads to Saru's psychological insecurity which finds release in two ways. One is through constant and recurrent dreams and the other is through acts of defiance. Her dreams mostly represent her guilt feelings. Therefore, she often dreams of Dhruva's death and the accusations made by her mother. In the words of Premila Paul: "She has always felt an inner drive to make him the mythological Dhruva (pushed off the father's lap by the step brother) and Dhruva in death becomes a tantalizing 'North Star' controlling her happiness from afar. The guilt had come to stay and she is destined to be in the dock perennially. Her husband, dead brother, dead mother and even her children are the accusers and she the accused." (67)

The acts of defiance mostly spring from her resentment against her mother and all that she stands for. She recollects her attitude towards her mother as a young girl, and then as a child, "I hated her, I wanted to hurt her, wound her, make her suffer." (142) She rebels against her mother by going to Bombay to study medicine and then later by marrying a man outside her caste. Saru's defiance can also be analyzed as an inherent quality present in her. As Premila Paul observes, "Saru is highly self-willed and her problems ensue because of her outsized ego and innate love for power over others." (61) She defies traditional codes at the slightest threat in her mother's house. If Mulk Raj Anand's Gauri in the novel, *The Old Woman and the Cow*, turns defiant because of the ill-treatment meted out to her by her husband, Saru's defiance is her second nature.

As a child, Saru also witnesses the dire straits of her grandmother who was deserted by her husband and considered a burden by her own people. This prompts her to seek economic independence as an insurance against subordination or suppression. And the events that follow in her life are mostly inspired by this goal. In her adolescence, in an impressionable frame of mind, Saru is attracted towards Manohar (called Manu), a fellow student in her college. Her senior by a few years, he is already a post-graduate student when she just enters college. He is quite popular in the college. He is not only good in his academic performance, but also active as the secretary of the Literary Association. He is actively associated with the Debating Union and he is the life and soul of the Dramatic Society. On top of all that, he is a budding writer and a poet of promise with some poems already published in magazines. He is, obviously, the heartthrob of many a girl student. Saru is introduced to Manu by her friend, Smita. Slipping into the first person narration, Shashi Deshpande makes her protagonist, Saru, describe herself in the most unflattering way in comparison to Padmini, the girl whom Manu is obviously attracted to. Saru recollects:

> That evening I went home and tried to imitate the way she had done her hair, and failed miserably. In a fury, I oiled my hair and slicked it into one tight plait and went to college knowing how unattractive I looked with my plump high cheeks, my oiled hair, my unpowdered face with its spattering of pimples. There was even, I remember, a kind of triumphant misery in knowing how awful I looked, how unlike, how terribly unlike his Padmini. (52)

She remains totally unacknowledged by the handsome Manu. A renewed acquaintance a few years later, however, leads the way to greater friendship and then to marriage. Saru is now a medical student in Bombay and Manu a lecturer in a local college.

Saru undergoes a great transformation after moving into the hostel on getting a seat in a medical college. After her conservative upbringing and the rigid atmosphere at home, she savours a sense of freedom for the first time in her life. She sheds some of her puppy fat and acquires a degree of sophistication in her cosmopolitan company and, on the whole, presents an attractive picture. Manu's interest in her, for the first time, makes her feel wanted and loved. It is this feeling which is partly responsible for making her rush into marriage with Manu. The other important reason is her defiant attitude. She defies her mother to join the medical college and now she defies her once more to marry out of her taste. In fact, she appears to take a vicious pleasure in deliberately going against her mother's rigid conservatism. She recalls the conversation with her mother when she confronts her with her intention of marrying Manu:

> "What caste is he?"
> "I don't know."
> "A Brahmin."
> "Of course, not."
> Then cruelly . . . "His father keeps a cycle shop."
> "Oh, so they are low-caste people, are they?"
> The word her mother had used, with the disgust, hatred and prejudice of centuries had so enraged her that she had replied . . . "I hope so." (96)

Years later Saru bitterly recollects that if her mother had not been so against him, perhaps, she would not have married him and landed herself in such a position. It had been her passionate desire to hurt her mother that made her rush headlong into marriage with Manu. In retrospection, she thinks:

> If you hadn't fought me so bitterly, if you hadn't been so against him, perhaps, I would never have married him. And I would not have been here, cringing from the sight of his hand-writing, hating him and yet pitying him too. (96)

But, in the first flush of her infatuation with Manohar, however, Saru considers herself highly privileged to have been chosen by him. Her craving for attention is fulfilled here and she wonders. "How could I be anyone's beloved? I was the redundant, the unwanted, an appendage one could do without." (66) She places him on a pedestal and all the other boys of her acquaintance seem to pale into insignificance in comparison to him. She thinks: "The fisherman's daughter couldn't have been more surprised when the king asked her to marry him, than I was by Manu's love for me." (66) Many years later, in a retrospective mood, however, she feels: "The fisherman's daughter was wiser. She sent the king to her father and it was the father who bargained with him, while I . . . I gave myself up unconditionally, unreservedly to him, to love him and to be loved." (66) All things considered, however, it only seems fair to admit that Saru's mother and father had important roles to play, each in his and her own way, in the factors that led to her marriage with Manu. If her mother had provoked her by her blatant hostility, her father had contributed to her present predicament by remaining a mute spectator in the family drama.

The initial years of her marriage are sheer bliss when she thinks that she is the luckiest woman on earth. As S.P. Swain observes, "She marries to attain autonomy of the self and to secure the lost love in her parental home. Manu is her saviour, the ideal romantic hero who rescues her from her insecure, wooden existence in her maternal home. Her marriage with Manu is an assertion on and affirmation of her feminine sensibility.[9] In her initial euphoric state, Saru thinks: "I was hungry for love. Each act of sex was a triumphant assertion of our love. Of my being loved. Of my being wanted." (40) Bound by her middle-class inhibitions, Saru does not permit herself any physical contact with Manu until they are married. But after her marriage, she revels in the act of love with a wild abandon:

> After the first moment of apprehension . . . a purely physical response, or lack of it, rather . . . there was never any withholding in me. I became in an instant a physically aroused woman with an infinite capacity for loving and giving, with a passionate desire to be absorbed by the man I loved. All the cliches, I discovered were true, kisses were soft and unbearably sweet, embraces hard and passionate, hands caressing and tender, and loving, as well as being

> loved was an intense joy. It was as if little nerve ends of pleasure had sprung up all over my body. (40)

She describes her dingy one-room apartment in which they first lived, as 'heaven on earth.' She is blissfully content in spite of "the corridors smelling of urine, the rooms with their dark sealed in odours, women with inquisitive, unfriendly eyes, men with lascivious stares." (40)

But happiness, as she soon discovers. is only an illusion and one is left with memories which are weighed with grief. As long as she is merely a medical student and her husband the bread-winner there is peace at home, even if 'home' is surrounded by filth and stench. The problems arise only when she gains recognition as a doctor. Saru remembers even the exact incident which becomes a turning point in their existence. Once, there is a fire accident in a factory near-by and she returns home late, in a stupour, after helping out the victims, still wearing her blood-stained coat. The news spreads in the neighbourhood that she is a doctor. Gradually people start paying more attention to her than previously. Her neighbours keep coming to her with sundry complaints, glad to have a doctor in their midst. Saru does not observe the slow change in her husband, in the initial exhilaration at her exalted status as a doctor. In a retrospective mood, much later, however, she is able to trace the events which lead to the disastrous condition of her marriage, saying: "He had been the young man and I his bride. Now I was the lady doctor and he was my husband." (42) This reversal of roles apparently is too much for Manu to accept. He gradually undergoes a change from that of a romantic hero quoting Shelley and Keats to his beloved, to a morose husband uncomfortable with his wife's steady rise in status.

In her new role as a career woman, Saru is no longer happy in their shabby apartment and prefers to move into something more decent. Until she starts earning, Saru seems quite content in the scrubby flat and somehow manages to live on Manu's salary which barely covers their expenses. But, eventually she begins to miss the small things that money can buy and resents

Manu's acceptance of such a kind of living:

> I had begun to wonder at his acceptance of our shabby way of living. For me, things now began to hurt . . . a frayed saree I could not replace, a movie I could not see, an outing I could not join in. I knew now that without money life became petty and dreary. The thought of going on this way became unbearable. (92)

Perhaps, life would have remained smooth and without turmoil had Saru restricted herself to being a doctor, treating the people around their shabby apartment. But, Saru aims higher and wants to specialize in order to achieve the things she dreams of. It is here that she makes use of Boozie to further her career. Boozie is described as an extrodinarily handsome, debonair and efficient doctor. He has a playboy image and Saru herself is surprised at his interest in her. She responds fittingly to his flirtatious manner and soon their relationship reaches a stage where Boozie helps her with enough money to set up her practice in a posh area. Shashi Deshpande very subtly hints at the feminine wiles employed by Saru in order to achieve certain things in life which otherwise may not have been possible. Saru stifles her scruples by telling herself, "I told myself my relationship with this man couldn't wouldn't hurt Manu, It was just a teacher-student relationship. If he put his hand on my shoulder, slapped me on my back held my hand or hugged me . . . that was just his mannerism and meant nothing. It had nothing to do with me and Manu." (91)

Strictly speaking, there is nothing 'physical' in Saru's affair with Boozie. To suit his own interests, Boozie openly flaunts his 'relationship' with Saru as a cover to his homosexuality. Saru on her part does nothing to clear this misconception in her husband's mind. In fact, she is slowly filled with such a loathing and contempt for her husband that she deliberately goads him into believing the obvious, as is evident from the conversation mentioned below:

> "I've got the money." [to open a consulting room] "How?" "Boozie gave it to me." He could have asked me then. . . . "Why?" And I would have told him. . . . What would I have said? But the occasion didn't arise because he never asked me. And there was, perversely no relief in me, but contempt that he didn't. (93)

Even when Boozie deliberately displays his affection for her in public before the staring eyes of all the invitees to the inauguration of her consulting room, Saru feels more resentful towards her husband than to him:

> I could feel the stares. Everyone's except Manu's who would not look at us. And I should have hated him then . . . not Manu, for he had done nothing then for which I could hate him, but this attractive, ravishingly masculine man who was doing this deliberately. Attracting attention to the two of us. But funnily enough, it was not him I hated, it was Manu for doing nothing. This man . . . no, I could not hate him knowing what I did about him. That behind the facade of aggressive, virile masculinity there was nothing at all. (94)

Gradually Saru's social and financial status grows far beyond that of her husband. She is a busy, successful doctor in contrast to Manu who is an underpaid lecturer in a third rate college. She establishes herself as a career woman and her profession satisfies her ego, but this brings her no happiness at home. Her predicament is contrary to the assertion of most feminists that economic independence brings fulfilment to the woman. Betty Friedan, for example, says: "For woman, as for man, the need for self-fulfilment—autonomy, self-realisation, independence, individuality, self-actualization is as important as the sexual need, with as serious consequences, when it is thwarted."[8]

Shashi Deshpande, however, proves that in the institution of marriage, an economically independent woman is still bound in shackles and must forever live in fear of hurting the ego of her husband. As Saru observes bitterly:

> a+b they told us in mathematics is equal to b+a. But here a+b was not, definitely not equal to b+a. It became a monstrously unbalanced equation, lopsided, unequal, impossible. (42)

With Saru's steady rise in status, the chasm, between her and Manu deepens and the marriage remains only a sham with Saru's growing reluctance to share physical intimacy with Manu. One particular incident comes to her mind when she tries to trace the events which led to her disillusionment with Manu:

> It had begun the day when the four of them had been watching a T.V programme. Manu had been sitting with his feet up on a stool, and unconsciously she stared at them . . . soft, white, unmarked and flabby. Like his hands. And his laugh . . . it was rather silly. A kind of bray almost. Why had she never noticed that before? And had he always picked at his ears that way, deftly, rather stealthily? She did not know how long she stared. It was like seeing a man she had never seen, never known. A man, whom, now that she knew him, she rather despised. (135)

The rift between Saru and her husband gradually grows wider, and one unfortunate incident blows the lid off the simmering pot. It changes Manu into a wild animal at night when he begins to physically abuse her in the privacy of their room. A girl who comes home to interview Saru for a magazine, innocently asks Manu: "How does it feel when your wife earns not only the butter but most of the bread as well?" (200) At that moment, Manu, Saru and the interviewer laugh over it as if it didn't matter. But later that night, Manu gives vent to his feelings by attacking her like a wild animal. The next morning he feigns complete ignorance of his own actions the previous night and appears normal in every way. The nightmarish incident recurs later in response to another similar, tactless remark made by Manu's colleague and his wife. Manu and Saru meet his colleague and his wife while shopping, prior to going on a vacation to a hill-station. Looking at the newly bought suitcase Manu's colleague asks them if they are going anywhere and Manu replies that they are going to Ooty and some places down South. The colleague comments that they are lucky to be able to afford such a trip and that he himself could not afford a much less expensive vacation. His wife replies tartly that he probably could have afforded it, had he married a doctor. An insulted Manu vents his frustration once more on Saru that night, making her a victim of his bestiality, as she later relates to her father:

> I never knew till then he had so much strength in him. . . . I couldn't fight back. I couldn't shout or cry, I was so afraid the children in the next room would hear. I could do nothing. I can never do anything. I just endure. (201)

The situation seems all the more terrible for Saru because Manu pretends that nothing has ever happened. He is perfectly normal in the mornings and goes about as if he was in total ignorance of his own actions. Unable to bear the torture any longer, Saru returns to her parents's home—a place she had vowed never to come back to. She is able to return partly because she knows her mother is dead and she will be spared the humiliation of putting up with her taunts, and partly because she is able to offer an immediate explanation to her father for her coming. She tells him that she has come to see him on hearing of her mother's death. Commending her on her description of the terrifying scene in bed, Premila Paul says: "married to a practising neuropathologist, Shashi Deshpande presumably has intimate knowledge of the neurotic world of the likes of Manu. But she shows remarkable restraint in the depiction of these scenes and spares readers the clinical details,." (64) Elsewhere a reviewer has commented on the use of pornography in the book: "Pornography is a convenient ploy for selling. But then Indian 'Moral consciousness' prevents pornographic fiction being accorded an honourable' literary reputation. In the circumstances how does an Indian writer resolve the problem of ensuring sales in a society where book buying is not a habit, and simultaneously preserve the hope of earning a reputable name? Shashi Deshpande devises her own answer. The first two pages of her recent novel *The Dark Holds Terrors* describe vividly, a scene of rape. It is printed in italics lest the reader should miss the import of such an epigraph. . . . A few paragraphs later, though, the writer sets the reader's conscience at rest by revealing the 'identity' of the rapist as the woman's husband; and since this woman's 'point-of-view' determines the action of the novel, the reader may look forward to further titillating scenes, all justifiable in the name of women's-lib. Thus prurient delights and the social theme are violently yoked together."[9]

Shashi Deshpande, in an interview with Lakshmi Holmstrom reacts to this observation saying: "I was astounded. Actually it didn't start for me, that novel, with the notion of rape, or sexual domination. It started with a couple, the uneasiness or tension between them. And I knew the man was not doing well in his career as the woman was, and I connected the two."[10]

It is easy to identify the consequences of the shattering of the male ego. Saru dwells upon this at length in her father's house and tries to objectively analyse her share of the blame in the disaster that her marriage has been. Her ruminations make her think, "My brother died because I heedlessly turned my back on him. My mother died alone because I deserted her. My husband is a failure because I destroyed his manhood." (217) Though this statement suggests a study in guilt consciousness, the novel in reality presents a stark picture of the gross inequalities prevailing in our society: gender discrimination by the parents towards their own children and the superiority of the male in a marriage, if it must survive.

When asked by her friend Nalu to talk on "Medicine as a profession for woman" to some college students, Saru makes up an imaginary speech which sarcastically sums up the conditions necessary for a successful marriage:

A wife must always be a few feet behind her husband. If

> he is an M.A., You should be a B.A. If he is 5'4" tall you shouldn't be more than 5'3" tall. If he is earning five hundred rupees, you should never earn more than four hundred and ninety, if you want a happy marriage. Don't ever try to reverse the doctor-nurse, executive-secretary, principal-teacher role. It can be traumatic, disastrous. And, I assure you, it is not worth it. He'll suffer. You'll suffer and so will the children. Women's magazines will tell you that a marriage must be an equal partnership. That's nonsense, rubbish. No partnership can ever be equal. It will always be unequal, but take care that it's unequal in favour of your husband. If the scales tilt in your favour, god help you, both of you. (137)

Saru's bitter realization is that a woman must necessarily remain a step behind her husband. Surprisingly enough, no less a person than John Ruskin holds a similar view: "A man ought to know any language or science he learns, thoroughly; while a woman ought to know the same language or science only so far as may enable her to sympathize in her husband's pleasures, and in those of his best friends."[11]

Looking back on her life, Saru also analyses her relationship with Padmakar, her classmate in medical college, whom she meets years later as a general practitioner. Padma, as he is called, is described as harmless and unassuming. He tries to forge a deeper friendship with Saru, but after a few meetings Saru dissuades him from doing so and brings an end to their relationship. She naively assumes that she would find comfort in this relationship, but is disappointed that it does not happen. She backs out eventually not because she is afraid of the consequences but because she has no illusions left about romance or love:

> Now I knew it was not just the consequences I feared and hated, but the thing itself, what had I imagined? Love? Romance? Both, I knew too well, were illusions and not relevant to my life anyway. And the code word of our age is

> neither love nor romance but sex. Fulfilment and happiness came, not through love alone, but sex. And for me, sex was now a dirty word. (133)

As Kamini Dinesh comments: In *The Dark Holds No Terrors* (also) there are other men but the relationship gives no solace. On the other hand, the homosexual Boozie and the frustrated Padma bring to Saru the disillusioning realization that there can be no happiness or fulfilment in these relationships. There cannot be an 'escape route' from the tension of married life. The woman seeking a crutch has, finally to fall back on herself."[12]

Shashi Deshpande also uses Saru's reunion with two of her school friends Smita and Nalu to contrast the lives of three women. One of them is Smita who leaves no opportunity to talk about her intimacy with her husband and spares no effort to present the picture of a happily married woman. She merely evokes the reader's pity and the contempt of her two friends. Her constant reference to HIM in her conversation provokes Nalu to comment: "There's always time to do all the things 'He' wants to do, you just tag on to him and drift, a small boat towed by a larger ship." (117)

Later referring to the change of her name at the time of her marriage from Smita to Anju (short for Gitanjali) by her husband, who is fond of Tagore, Nalu asks her with contempt, "Do you have to surrender so easily?" (117) She refuses to be taken in by Smita's coy references to her husband, her simpering attitude and her obvious desire to please his every whim. She contemptuously tells her, "Well, I refuse to call you Anju or Gitanjali or whatever. To me you are Smita and will always be Smita." (118) When Smita asks Saru for a small loan to buy a saree for her sister-in-law without her husband's knowledge, it makes Saru despise the fact of her complete dependence on her husband for money. Smita envies the economic independence of Nalu and Saru.

Nalu's life as a spinster does not seem very enviable either. She is a lecturer and lives with her brother and his family. She has acquired an air of dignity and confidence, "but with it a conviction of her own rightness that made her seem overbearing and dogmatic." (121) Saru observes the bitterness that has creeped into her and contrasts it with the Nalu of her college days who had been full of enthusiasm. She refuses, however, to accept the seemingly obvious reason of her spinsterhood for her bitterness. The character of Nalu brings to mind the words of Betty Friedan, who, in her book *The Feminine Mystique*, writes: "The first women in business and the professions were thought to be freaks, insecure in their new freedom, some perhaps feared to be soft or gentle, love, have children, lest they lose their prized independence, lest they be trapped again as their mothers were." (89)

Trying to analyse the change in Nalu, Saru thinks that it would be foolish to "say that she [Nalu] is bitter because she never married? never bore a child. But that would be as stupid as calling me fulfilled because I got married and I have borne two children." (121) Through the lives of Smita and Nalu, Saru is able to contrast the joys and sorrows of a wife and mother and that of a spinster. She finds that it is difficult to draw conclusions and say who is happier and more fulfilled. As Betty Friedan observes: "Of the growing thousands of women currently getting private psychiatric help in the United States, the married ones were reported dissatisfied with their marriages, the unmarried ones suffering from anxiety and, finally depression." (23) She, however, continues: "Strangely a number of psychiatrists stated that, in their experience unmarried women patients were happier than married ones." (23)

Shashi Deshpande tries to repudiate the myth that women find fulfilment only in marriage. She, however, does not go to the other extreme of proclaiming that all unmarried women are destined to be happy. Her objectivity has, in fact, prompted reviewers to commend her. Premila Paul observes: "Shashi Deshpande does not glorify women's sufferings. Though she enlists a sufficient amount of sympathy for her protagonist, it is not on the grounds of her being a female sufferer. Throughout the novel Shashi Deshpande maintains commendable objectivity and avoids generalizations and partial views." (69)

There are some reviewers, nevertheless, who have referred to *The Dark Holds No Terrors* as a feminist work, first because the novel is written by a contemporary woman novelist and second, because the protagonist in it is a woman and, therefore, the novel is replete with her experiences, her feelings and her observations, invoking a certain amount of sympathy towards her on the part of the reader. It would not be fair, however, to classify the book as such on such flimsy grounds. Shashi Deshpande clarifies that she has chosen to have a woman as a central character not in order to project or support some feminist position because she feels that she can write about a woman with conviction and some inner knowledge. She says: "I know women better than I know men, so perhaps my books are more about women, and that's about it."[13] She also talks about the reluctance of some women to be identified as women writers:

> Some women writers say that they don't want to be called women writers. I think it's wrong. Because I think by saying so, you're saying there's something wrong in being a woman writer, something inferior or subordinate in being called a woman writer. So I don't want to do that either. I am a woman and I do write about women, and I am going to say it loudly. I don't want to dissociate myself, which is like saying, "Look, that's an inferior kind of a club, and I don't want to be part of it."[14]

But, irrespective of the fact whether she has consciously written a feminist novel or not, there is a strong note of protest in her book, not only in the voice of her protagonist about her own life but also in her observation about the other characters in the novel. One incident which remains firmly implanted in the reader's mind is that of the visit paid by Saru and Manohar to the latter's friend's house. They are invited to tea. Manohar's friend talks to them while his wife unobtrusively moves around, serving the eats, the tea and glasses of water. Her husband totally ignores her presence and so do his guests. While going home, Saru goes in to take care of her and smiles at her but receives no response.

> Her face was unchanged, expressionless as if she had fallen in with her husband's desires and successfully effaced the person that was her. At the door I looked back for a moment, she stood under a light, a strong, unshaded bulb hanging low in the centre of the room. I looked down at her feet and saw that there was no shadow. For some reason, the words came to my mind if I cast no shadow, I do not exist. (159)

Elsewhere, Saru's observations as a lady doctor and her contempt for martyred women suffering silently underline her feminist ideas:

> The myriad complaints, the varying symptoms, she thought, if put together would provide a world of data for a treatise on the condition of women. Backache, headache, leucorrhea, menorrhea, loss of appetite, burning feet, an itch 'there' . . . all the indignities of a woman's life borne silently and as long as possible, because "how do you tell anyone about these things?"
>
> Everything kept secret, their very womanhood a source of deep shame to them. Stupid, silly martyrs, she thought, idiotic heroines going on with their tasks, and destroying themselves in the bargain, for nothing but a meaningless modesty. Their unconscious, unmeaning heroism born out of the myth of the self-sacrificing martyred woman, did not arouse her pity or her admiration. (107)

Statements like this leave one in no doubt about the writer's feminist stance. Shashi Deshpande, nonetheless, maintains that she has never consciously projected any feminist ideas. Her novels and short stories which contain feminist thought—women's sexuality, the construction of gender roles as wives and mother, self-discoveries, lead interviewers to ask the inevitable question as to what extent she would consider herself a feminist. Her reply is very simple:

> I now have no doubts at all in saying that I am a feminist. In my life, I mean. But not consciously as a novelist. I must also say that my feminism has come to me very slowly, very gradually and mainly out of my own thinking and experiences and feelings. I started writing first and only then discovered my feminism. And it was much later that I actually read books about it.[15]

Most feminist writers in Indian languages hold almost the same view. C.S. Laxmi (Ambai), the Tamil writer expresses a similar opinion when she says, "I also don't sit down and tell myself that I am going to write a feminist story. Feminism is part of my life, it's what I am."[16] Nevertheless, reviewers like Malashri Lal are not convinced by Shashi Deshpande's statement that she is not a consciously feminist novelist. She thinks that she shares "her protagonist's conviction that women are God's and society's cruelly wronged creatures." (170) They contend that *The Dark Holds No Terrors* contains several scenes—in a village, in a college cafeteria, in Bombay chawls, in a bed room, in maternity wards—where women are denied the right to be individuals. They say that feminist slogans scream out of every few pages and become unified in a convenient paragraph at the end:

> They came to her then, all those selves she had rejected so resolutely at first and so passionately later. The guilty sister, the undutiful daughter, the unloving wife . . . all persons spiked with guilts. Yes, she was all of them, she could not deny that now. She had to accept these selves to become whole again. (201)

Shashi Deshpande, however, feels that her brand of feminism, if it must be called so, is not the militant feminism adopted by Western writers. The problems of her protagonists rise mostly from situations in the Indian context and differ from those of their Western counterparts. She does not think it necessary to refer to Western feminist ideology in her novels and regrets the fact that many in our country have no clear idea of the concept of feminism. In an interview to Lakshmi Holmstrom, Deshpande says:

> It is difficult to apply Kate Millett or Simone De Beauvoir or whoever to the reality of our daily lives in India. And often there are such terrible misconceptions about feminism by people here. They often think it is about burning bras and walking out on your husband, children or about not having children etc. I always try to make the point now about what feminism is not and to say that we have to discover what it is in our own lives, our experiences. And I actually feel that a lot of women in India are feminists without realizing it. (26)

Other critics like R. Mala who interpret extra-marital relationship as part of feminism say that the sexually repressed Deshpande's women "strive for expression through sexual relationships or affairs with men other than their husbands. Saru's affair with Boozie (her boss) and Padmakar Rao (her collegemate) seem temporary substitutes for her unfulfilled marital life."[17] This is certainly reading beyond the text. A close study of the novel reveals that Saru does not indulge in any physical relationship either with Boozie or with Padmakar Rao, and so the question of being unfaithful or having an extra-marital affair does not arise. On the contrary, Saru seems to have lost interest in sex after the nightly assaults of her husband, Manu. This is made clear when she says: "And for me sex was now a dirty word." (133) R. Mala's presumption that an educated woman, who tries to assert herself as an individual, must necessarily be promiscuous is typical of the thinking of most of the Indians.

Like Mulk Raj Anand, Shashi Deshpande also protests against the labelling of her work as 'propagandist.' She vehemently denies any such attempt on her part. In her interview to Sue Dickman, she says, "Somebody once asked me if I have a social purpose in my writing and I very loudly said no, I have no social purpose. I write because it comes to me." (34) In another interview to Stanley Carvalho, she says:

> I hate to write propagandist literature. I think good literature and propaganda do not go together. Any literature written with some viewpoint of proving something rarely turns out to be good literature. Literature comes very spontaneously and when I write I am concerned with people.[18]

She elaborates her point further when she says:

> Perhaps, being a woman, I find myself sympathizing with women. If others see something feminist in my writings, I must say that it is not consciously done. It is because the world for women is like that and I am mirroring the world. I find a lot of men unsympathetic to my writing and a lot of women extremely sympathetic. This is because the world is viewed in different ways by men and women.

The Dark Holds No Terrors has an open ending. Saru, during her brief stay in her father's house, receives many letters from her husband which remain unanswered, as she is still in an undecided state. Towards the end of the novel, however, Saru receives a telegram and prepares herself to confront Manu. There can be no definite meanings read into such an ending. It is clear that she will no longer remain an object for Manu to vent his frustration. Though the novel has an open ending, the reader is left in no doubt as to the intentions of the novelist. As R. Mala remarks: "The novelist's credo is to 'take refuge in the self which means that the self is not metaphysical but psychological. In other words, Deshpande means that the heroines will in future assert themselves; they will no longer allow their 'she' to get deceased. By this assertion of the self, Deshpande certainly takes her heroines to the pole of feminism though she may not have aimed at propounding such an 'ism.'" (56-57) From this critical comment, it is clear that Saru is fully determined to take control over her life by shedding her passivity.

N O T E S

1. Shashi Deshpande, *The Dark Holds No Terrors* (New Delhi: Penguin, 1990).
2. Ragini Ramachandra, Rev. of *The Dark Holds No Terrors*, *The Literary Criterion*, Vol. XXI, Nos. 1 & 2, 1986, 120.
3. Sarabjit Sandhu, "*The Dark Holds No Terrors*," *Image of Woman in the Novels of Shashi Deshpande* (New Delhi: Prestige, 1991), 20.
4. Premila Paul, "*The Dark Holds No Terrors*; A Woman's Search for Refuge," *Indian Women Novelists*, ed. R.K. Dhawan (New Delhi: Prestige, 1991), Set I, Vol. V, 67.
5. Mrinal Pande, *Daughter's Daughter* (New Delhi: Penguin, 1994).
6. S. Anandalakshmi, "The Female Child in a Family Setting," *The Indian Journal of Social Work*, Vol. LII, No. 1, Jan. 1991, 31.
7. S.P. Swain, "Shashi Deshpande's *The Dark Holds No Terrors*: Saru's Feminine Sensibility," *Indian Women Novelists*, Vol. IV, 35-36.
8. Betty Freidan, *The Feminine Mystique* (Harmondsworth: Penguin, 1971), 282.
9. Malashri Lal, "Goodluck to Entrepreneurs," Rev. of *The Dark Holds No Terrors*, *Indian Book Chronicle*, Vol. 6, No. 9, May 16, 1981, 169.
10. Lakshmi Holmstrom, "Shashi Deshpande Talks to Lakshmi Holmstrom," *Wasafiri*, No. 17, Spring, 1993, 23.
11. *Sesame and Lilies*, Quoted in Kate Millett, *Sexual Politics* (1969; rpt. London: Rupert Hart-Davis, 1971), 74.
12. Kamini Dinesh, "Moving Out of the Cloistered Self: Shashi Deshpande's Protagonists," *Margins of Erasure: Purdah in the Sub-Continental Novel in English*, ed. Jasbir Jain and Amina Amin (New Delhi: Sterling, 1995), 200.
13. Sue Dickman, "In Conversation: Sue Dickman with Indian Women Writers," *The Book Review*, Vol. 19, No. 4, Apr. 1995, 32.
14. *Ibid.*, 32.
15. *Ibid.*, 34.
16. *Ibid.*, 34.
17. Mala, "Sexual Predicament and Shashi Deshpande's Women," *Indian Women Novelists*, Set I, Vol. V, 56.
18. Stanley Carvalho, "Everyone has a Right to Choose a Language," *The Sunday Observer*, No. 11, Feb. 1990.

"Silent No More": *That Long Silence*

> I myself have never been able to find out precisely what feminism is: I only know that people call me a feminist whenever I express sentiments that differentiate me from a doormat.
>
> Rebecca West, 1913

> If I were a man and cared to know the world I lived in I almost think it would make me a shade uneasy, the weight of that long silence.
>
> Elizabeth Robins

Shashi Deshpande derives the title of her novel, *That Long Silence*, from the classic understatement by Elizabeth Robins made in a speech to a world body. This long silence was unfortunately punctured by a few early women writers who did not present facts as they were preferring, instead, to dwell on superficial matters and more often than not, churning out mushy, sentimental romances which had no connection with reality. And, the few women writers who tried to present facts from the woman's point of view often succumbed to the feminist ideology of creating strong women characters. This again tended to distort the truth in as much a manner as the writing by men did.

Judged against this backdrop, *That Long Silence* comes relatively close to real life experience. The novel achieves greater credibility from the fact that Jaya, the protagonist, is a very well-read person, possessing a literary sensitivity which corresponds with her fictional role. Often, in spite of the writer's best efforts the narrator fails to find a voice of her own and ends up mouthing the creator. Articulate women characters are obviously difficult to create, nurtured as they are in the culture of silence. The author has managed to overcome this difficulty by endowing her protagonist with abundant creative talent. In the words of Vimala Rama Rao, "Jaya is one of the rare narrative voices in Indian English fiction who possesses and displays a literary sensibility commensurate with her fictional role as a writer telling her own story, one whose college education and reading habits are in evidence in her speaking voice. This indeed is an achievement."[1] Greatly conscious of the stifling social milieu, the narrator/writer unfolds her story "Ostensibly, she relates it as the story of a particular couple, but the power relations in the patriarchal structure, the gender differentiation with all its ramifications, and the typical travails of the woman struggling to define herself take on the dimension of the condition and place of the Indian woman in society."[2]

That Long Silence portrays the conflict in the mind of the narrator between the writer and the housewife. For seventeen long years, Jaya manages to suppress her feelings, thinking that it is more important to be a good wife than a good writer. She perhaps would have remained in the shadow of her husband, Mohan, for the rest of her life if it had not been for the jolt received to the carefully constructed edifice of her family. A crisis is sparked off by her husband's involvement in a shady deal. There are charges of corruption against him and it is expected that an enquiry will be conducted. He feels consoled to some extent that the children Rahul and Rati are away on a long tour with their family friends. He takes it for granted that his wife will go along with him into hiding. Jaya follows her husband into exile as unhesitatingly as her mythological counterpart Sita displaying her '*Sati-dharma*.'

In the silence of their Dadar flat where they have shifted temporarily and in the absence of her usual domestic routine. Jaya goes into an intense introspection of her life. After seventeen years of playing out her many-faceted role of a loyal wife and tireless mother, the silence becomes deafening. Jaya's loneliness is further accentuated as she ponders over the intrinsic isolation of the human condition. Jaya appears to be a satisfied housewife married to an apparently caring man and having two normal, healthy children. Ensconced in a comfortable home, without any dearth of material comforts, Jaya seems to lead an enviable life by any standards. However, a closer scrutiny of her life, as gleaned from the retrospective account of her marriage, reveals that to achieve this stage of fulfilment as a wife, Jaya has systematically suppressed many traits of her personality that could not fit her role as wife and mother. The two most striking things she had to suppress were her writing career and her association with Kamat, her neighbour at one time.

In the early years of her marriage, Jaya is on the threshold of acquiring a name as a creative writer of some merit. One of her short stories bags the first prize and is published in a magazine. Mohan, who earlier tolerates her writing as something quite harmless and even takes pride in being the husband of a writer, displays an insensitivity and intolerance about a particular short story written by his wife. The story in question is about "a couple, a man who cannot reach out to his wife except through her body."[3] Mohan thinks that the story portrays their own personal life, and he is very apprehensive of the idea that the people of his acquaintance may assume that he is the kind of person portrayed in the story. This is enough to jeopardize Jaya's career as a writer. Though she knows that there is no truth in what her husband thinks, she does not try to reason with him. She thinks, "Looking at his stricken face, I had been convinced. I had done him wrong. And I had stopped writing after that." (144) She begins to write under an assumed name. But her stories are rejected by one publisher after another. Once while trying to analyse the reason behind the series of rejections, her neighbour, Kamat, after reading the rejected stories, tells her that they are devoid of any strong emotion since she has carefully censored all the anger from the story making it impersonal and shorn of a personal vision. Jaya argues with Kamat that it is not a womanly trait to show anger. Here she is merely repeating the words used by her husband on the occasion of their first quarrel after marriage. She asserts, "A woman can never be angry. She can only be neurotic, hysterical, frustrated." (147) Kamat refuses to pamper her mood of self-pity and admonishes her instead: "Beware of this 'women are the victims' theory of yours. It will drag you down into a soft, squishy bog of self-pity. Take yourself seriously, woman. Don't skulk behind a false name." (148)

Jaya later starts writing light, humorous pieces on the travails of a middle-class housewife in a column titled "Seeta." This receives a good response from the editors and readers and, more importantly, gets a nod of approval from her husband, Mohan. Jaya states:

> Seeta had been the means through which I had shut the door firmly on all these women who had invaded my being, screaming for attention; women I had known I could not write about, because they might, it was just possible, resemble Mohan's mother or aunt or my mother or aunt. (149)

The statement effectively conveys the fact that women writers have all along abstained from telling the truth, giving greater credence to their roles as wives than to themselves as individuals. Kamat, as a hard critic, is contemptuous of such writing, knowing full well that Jaya is capable of writing better stuff. He frankly tells her: "I can never imagine you writing this. This you, I mean. I can see the woman who writes this. She's plump, good humoured, pea brained, but shrewd, devious, skimming over life." (149) As Adele King observes: "In a self-referential parody, Deshpande makes Jaya a writer of woman's magazine fiction. In Jaya's stories they lived happily ever after although she knows the falsity of the view of life. Also, the mixture of surrealism and fantasy in some of the experiences the writer undergoes is an important aspect of the making and unmaking of fictions in *That Long Silence*."[4]

The other most important aspect of Jaya's personality which clashes with her image of wife and mother, is her association with Kamat, who is a widower and lives in an apartment above Jaya's flat at Dadar He is a lonely man and showers his attention on Jaya. He is totally unlike most other men Jaya has known in the sense that he has no reservations about doing things like cooking which are usually considered to be a woman's domain. She feels totally at ease in his company because he treats her as an equal. She is not made to suffer any condescension as in the company of other men. In his company, she rids herself of all her inhibitions and opens up to him all her problems. He, however, refuses to let her wallow in self-pity. Instead, he analyses situations objectively and rationally without offering her the luxury of burrowing in false sympathy. He is an advertiser by profession and is apparently well read. He is able to offer constructive criticism to Jaya with regard to her writing. He understands her fears and even volunteers to receive her mail at his address, so that she could avoid a confrontation with her husband who disapproves of her writing.

The initial platonic nature of their relationship develops into physical attraction in course of time. She is more uninhibited in his company than in that of her husband. Her relationship with him cannot be placed into a particular category. At one moment he chides her like a father and the next moment he compliments her like a lover. He makes some personal remarks which are not usually made by men to women who are not their wives or lovers. For instance, he says: "I prefer clean, spare lines in a human being. You, for example—your name is like your face." (152) Once in a particularly emotional moment when she recalls her father's death, she finds herself in his arms as he attempts to console her. She responds to his touch and comes close to surrendering her body. Later, recounting the experience she thinks: "There had been nothing but an overwhelming urge to respond to him with my body, the equally overwhelming certainty of my mind that I could not do so." (157)

In spite of the willingness of her body and the ample opportunity provided in the seclusion of his apartment, Jaya overcomes her yearning in the interest of safeguarding her marriage. The man-woman relationship, going by the norms of society, is dictated by deceit and treachery. Human beings, more often than not, prefer to go by the dictates of society rather than be truthful to themselves as individuals. Appearances have to be maintained at any cost. It is, perhaps, this which prompts Jaya to behave in an utterly callous way on the death of Kamat. On one of her visits to his room, Jaya finds Kamat lying dead on the floor of his flat. She is unable to pay homage to her friend for the fear of getting involved in any scandal which might endanger her marriage. A terrible feeling of guilt envelops her, but she remains helplessly passive. According to Sarla Palkar, "She, perhaps does her role of wife to perfection, but fails as a human being."[5] Through this incident, Shashi Deshpande also highlights the plight of the so-called educated women still bound firmly by the shackles of tradition and convention. As G.D. Barche observes: "Unhesitatingly the modern educated young woman's crusade against years of slavery, suffering and suppression is a serious one. However, in the process of this crusade, we see her suffering from certain weaknesses and complexes which have been highlighted by the Indian women novelists. The first weakness she suffers from can be summed up in what Pope has said of Addison 'Willing to wound, yet afraid to strike.'"[6]

Though her creative writing and her close association with Kamat are two glaring examples of Jaya's inability to seek her own identity, there are several other factors which hinder her development as a complete individual in her own right. In her anxiety to perform her role as a perfect wife and a loving and caring mother, her identity is relegated to the background. Her name 'Jaya' which is given to her at birth by her parents is changed to 'Suhasini' at the time of marriage. To please her husband, she transforms her appearance to suit his idea of a modern woman. She cuts her hair, wears dark glasses and ultimately gets so completely absorbed into the family fold that from a fiercely independent woman she is transformed into the "sterotype of a woman: nervous, incompetent, needing male help and support?" (76) She proves that "Subtle indoctrination atrophies woman's desires to change her position as an object and to exercise her free will. She compromises her stand for she is taught the importance and necessity of stable marriage and family—family as security, as a source of emotional strength."[7] She desperately clings on to her husband as if her life depends on it. At times, she is beset with the fear that something may happen to Mohan:

> The thought of living without him had twisted my insides, his death had seemed to me the final catastrophe. The very idea of his dying had made me feel so bereft that tears had flowed effortlessly down my cheeks. If he had been a little late coming home, I had been sure he was dead. By the time he returned, I had, in my imagination shaped my life to a desolate widowhood. (96-97)

Jaya is a representative of the urban, middle-class woman exposed to liberal Western ideas. But she is unable to free herself entirely from the clutches of male chauvinist ideas. These ideas are a part and parcel of her culture, thrust upon her by those around her. Her aunt, Vanita *Mami*, for instance, counsels her just before her wedding: "Remember Jaya, a husband is like a sheltering tree. Keep the tree alive and flourishing, even if you have to water it with deceit and lies." (32) Vanita *Mami*'s long suffering role of a martyred wife prompts Jaya at one time before her marriage to think that, maybe, she too had been similarly counselled as a bride, "If your husband has a mistress or two, ignore it. Take up a hobby instead, cats, maybe, or your sister's children." (32) In spite of her flippant attitude towards Vanita Mami's advice, however, Jaya proves that she is no different from her. When it comes to the question of a choice between her husband and family, and asserting herself as an independent individual, she chooses the former without hesitation.

The sudden catastrophe of the corruption charges against Mohan and their exile to the Dadar flat, however, compel Jaya to "excavate her own truths and those of the other women in her life and unlock *That Long Silence*."[8] In contrast to her mythical counterpart and the Indian model of womanhood, Sita, Jaya is not wholly willing to sneak away like a thief into hiding with her husband, unquestioningly. The subtle sense of shame which pervades her being is enough to provoke an outburst from her husband. He tries to defend himself saying, 'It was for you and the children that I did this. I wanted you to have a good life, I wanted the children to have all those things I never had." (9)

Through this episode of corruption, we also get a glimpse of the Indian concept of ethics. Mohan, as viewed by the Indian standards, is a dutiful son and by extension, a dutiful husband and father. He regularly sends money to his family and attends the death anniversary of his father, bearing the expenditure involved. He accepts illegal gratification so that his family can move into a posh flat and live in comfort. Shashi Deshpande makes a relevant point in this context which hints at the casual way in which the code of morality is flouted by Indians to whom, "Dishonesty, nepotism and corruption, as they are understood in the West, are merely abstract concepts."[9]

In the small, drab flat at Dadar, Jaya's carefully built facade cracks and she breaks her self-imposed silence. She proceeds to unmask layer by layer the superficial aspects of her married life to reveal the hard core of reality. As Indira Bhatt observes, "Shashi Deshpande unmasks both Jaya and Mohan when they face the crisis in their lives. They have run into stormy weather and their secure sheltered life washes away like a water colour in a rainy storm."[10] Each of them reacts to the crisis in a different manner. Mohan becomes restless and unsettled, away from his routine work. He feels insecure and confused. He expects his wife to empathize with him because he feels he has got involved in this mess only because of her and the children. What is more, he wishes to use his wife "as a buffer, an opiate to soften the impact of the forces he has set into motion against himself. In fact, he is seeking emotional gratification for his insecurity created by his own deeds. He wants to hold hard to Jaya in whom he seeks an anchor in this tempest."[11]

But Jaya herself faces a traumatic situation. She too has been jolted out of a false complacence. Ever since her marriage she had been content to follow the footsteps of the mythological role model of Sita. At one time, she even tried to emulate the mythical Gandhari: "If Gandhari, who bandaged her eyes to become blind like her husband could be called an ideal wife, I was an ideal wife too. I bandaged my eyes tightly. I didn't want to know anything. It was enough for me that we moved to Bombay;

that we could send Rahul and Rati to good schools, that I could have the things we needed—decent clothes, a fridge, a gas connection, travelling I class." (61-62)

Looking up to her husband as a 'sheltering tree,' she had been lulled into a false sense of security. Whatever chaotic conditions prevailed outside, a home is a safe and secure place with the husband as the head of the family. This sense of security is shattered with the sudden prospect of Mohan facing an enquiry. Added to this is the weight of her husband's insecurity, fear and feeling of inadequacy that she has to put up with. It is the height of irony that when she desperately needs a shoulder to lean on, Jaya is accused by her husband of avoiding him. Mohan, seeking the unstinting support of his wife, cringes under the subtle hint of withdrawal by Jaya. He feels cheated by her failure to communicate with him on this issue. At one point he bursts out:

> I've always put you and the children first. I have been patient with all your whims, I have grudged you nothing. But the truth is that you despise me because I have failed. As long as I had my job and position, it was alright. But now because I am likely to lose it all . . . (12)

After sometime, he continues accusingly: "Do you think I haven't seen how changed you are since we came here, since I told you about my situation." (12) A hysterical Jaya bursts out laughing at this outburst from Mohan. She herself cannot understand what provokes the laughter but she is unable to stop herself. This is the last straw for Mohan who leaves the house in a huff in a seemingly permanent way. His absence unnerves her and she thinks her world will fall apart.

To add to her despair, Jaya gets the news that her son Rahul, who had been holidaying with their family friends, has suddenly disappeared. This piece of news shatters her and hits her with the force of a bolt striking a tender tree. Later Rahul returns and she receives a telegram from Mohan that 'All is well.' Before this happens, however, she lives for several days in a traumatic state. Her thoughts go back and forth in time, triggered by the slightest provocation in the present. There is no one she can turn to in her despair. She struggles alone with the trauma, and though it upsets her mental equilibrium, she emerges victorious. When she finally comes out of her emotional upheaval, she comes to terms with herself and her position. For the two nights before the return of her son and husband that she has to herself in the Dadar flat, she pours out her innermost thoughts, giving vent to her pent up feelings, her fears, her doubts and everything she had suppressed in her seventeen years of silence. As Subhash Chandra comments, "By permitting her story, she has achieved articulation of her predicament, her constraints, her anguish and has thereby broken her silence." (155) In this cathartic state, a realization dawns on her:

> The panic has gone. I am Mohan's wife. I had thought, and cut off the bits of me that had refused to be Mohan's wife. Now I know that kind of a fragmentation is not possible. (191)

She rejects the persistent image of "two bullocks yoked together." (7) She recollects that while studying Sanskrit she had learnt with outrage that women characters were not allowed to speak Sanskrit and had to use Prakrit. She realizes now that she had been speaking Prakrit all along. She resolves to "plug that hole in the heart," and to speak as well as listen, in order to erase the silence. After her purgation, "Jaya no longer wants to play the role of a passive wife. Perhaps, this is the hardness and ruthlessness that Deshpande talks about in the foreword. A man is conditioned to it right from the beginning, a woman learns through experience."[12]

The novel that is finally written by Jaya contains not only her story and that of her husband and children but numerous other characters, mostly Kusum, her mad cousin, Mohan's mother and many other victims like them—"Victims of patriarchy and also of their own silence."[13] Jaya tries to define herself negatively through the insanity of her cousin, Kusum, a deserted wife. Since she had always been paired with Kusum in her parental home at Ambegaon, Jaya defines herself as not Kusum: "But Kusum was nuts, thank god, Kusum, you are nuts, I had thought complacently; because you are nuts, I know I am sane." (126)

Jaya keeps the insane Kusum at home and takes care of her in spite of strong objections from her mother and brothers. After recovering a bit, she is taken home by her brother, Dilip. She, however, commits suicide a day before her husband is supposed to take her home. In a letter informing Jaya of the death, her mother writes: "But it was a good thing in a way. She was of no use to anyone after she went crazy, nobody needed her." (22)

Jaya tears the letter furiously. She recollects bitterly how Dilip, Kusum's matric-failed brother, "a detestable brash boy," (22) is idolized and his failure is made a positive qualification. His mother boasts, "Our Dilip is a non-matric," (22) and that as a union leader in a factory he is paid black money to keep him quiet. Kusum on the other hand is considered dispensable.

A close study of *That Long Silence* reveals that it abounds in incidents which highlight the gross inequalities between the sexes. The story of Mohan's mother as retold by Mohan and his sister, Vimala, is particularly poignant. Mohan's mother was a professional cook who earned money cooking for wedding feasts. She used to get beaten up by her husband frequently. The husband would come late, usually after a drinking bout but the rice had to be served steaming hot to him from a vessel which had not been touched by anyone else. Mohan's mother, of course, would eat after him. Mohan tells Jaya about one incident when his father returned home late one night to find that there was no *chutney* to eat along with his rice. He flung the plate against the wall and walked off. Mohan's mother sent him to the neighbour's house to borrow chillies, prepared *chutney* and fresh rice and waited huddled near the fireside until her husband returned at midnight. Relating the story years later to Jaya, Mohan exclaims, "God, she was tough, women in those days were tough." (36) Looking at it from a woman's point of view, Jaya writes:

> He saw strength in the woman sitting silently in front of

> the fire, but I saw despair. I saw a despair so great that it would not voice itself. I saw a struggle so bitter that silence was the only weapon. Silence and surrender. (36)

A few of Jaya's recollections turn morbid at times. For instance, the description of Mohan's mother's death. Mohan's sister Vimala describes the scene graphically to her sister-in-law, Jaya, something which she was unable to discuss with her own brother:

> I was collecting my books when suddenly the thump of her hands as she beat out the *bhakries* came to a stop. I thought it was the usual pause between two *bhakries* and I didn't bother until I heard her screams. I didn't even imagine it was her screaming at first, it was not like her voice at all. It was a thin ugly voice that scared me to death. And then as I watched, she began hitting herself on the face. Her hands were all floury, and wet too, and her face soon became white and floury, soon there were red patches as she went on and on hurting herself . . . There was ash from the fireplace on her hair and all that flour on her face—her face was swollen by now. With her eyes caved in she looked like a dead person, her face was the face of a dead woman. A week later she died. She went to a midwife and tried to get herself aborted. (38)

Looking at the framed photographs of Mohan's parents in his brother's house, Jaya thinks, "The mother looks like any other woman of her time, staring blank-faced at the world, the huge *kum-kum* on her forehead blotting out everything in that face but the blessed woman who died with her husband yet living." (38) A generation later, Mohan's sister Vimala, too, who is the victim of ovarian tumour, bleeds herself to death in silence rather than inform her mother-in-law about it. She, of course, realizes that it would be of no use to do so. Her mother-in-law's response to her illness confirms this: "God knows what's wrong with her. She's been lying there on her bed for over a month now. Yes, take her away if you want to. I never heard of women going to hospitals and doctors for such a thing. As if other women don't have heavy periods. What a fuss. But these women who have never had any children are like that." (39) We may say that this is a typically conditioned response in a patriarchal system.

Jeeja, Jaya's maid-servant, is another typical example of the oppressed woman. She is battered about by her good-for-nothing drunken husband. Without a murmur of protest, she supports him and even provides him liquor with her hard-earned money. She bears no grudge against him even when he takes up another woman. She justifies it by saying, "God didn't give us any children. That was his misfortune as well as mine. How could I blame him for marrying again when I couldn't give him any children?" (52) After the death of her husband and his mistress, she willingly brings up their son, Rajaram, who is a chip of the old block. He drinks and beats up his wife, Tara. Jeeja, however, does not allow Tara to even abuse or curse her husband. She admonishes her saying, "Stop that, don't forget, he keeps the *kumkum* on your forehead. What is a woman without that?" (53) Subhash Chandra comments about Jeeja: "Manu could not have hoped for a more steadfast follower." (152) There is also the character of Jaya's grandmother, *Ajji*, who, once widowed, takes to an empty room, never to emerge again, and that of Mukta and Vanita *Mami*. Mukta is Jaya's immediate neighbour at her Dadar flat. She is widowed at a young age and lives with her parents and a rebellious daughter, Nilima. She is the sort who will go out of the way, to help people. She is deeply pious and Jaya cannot help but wonder at the utter uselessness of such self-torture, "If it wasn't 'her Saturday' it was 'her Monday' or 'her Thursday.' Mukta had more days of fasts than days on which she could eat a normal meal. Her self-mortification seemed to be the most positive thing about her. And yet her piety—surely it was that which prompted those fasts—seemed meaningless, since she had already forfeited the purpose of it, the purpose of all Hindu women's fasts—the avoidance of widowhood." (67) Jaya's barren Vanita *Mami* too would perform numerous *pujas* and fasts in the hope of being blessed with a child, "but she had gone on with her fasts, her ritual circumambulations of the *Tulsi* plant, of the Peepul tree, even when their aim had gone beyond her reach, when her uterus had shrivelled and her ovaries atrophied." (67)

Individual tragedies of several women known to Jaya are woven into the tapestry of the novel written supposedly of herself and Mohan. It is this which makes *That Long Silence* stand out as a feminist novel, in spite of the author's reluctance to be branded a feminist writer. Several reviews of the novel bear testimony to this view which emphasizes the fact that the central theme in *That Long Silence* is to highlight the grossly unequal status of women in our society. For instance, Tapan Basu says that this novel is the story of Jaya, "who has spent a lifetime in surrender of her will to social mores and customs that had relegated women to a second class status."[14] Going through the various interviews given by Deshpande as well as by the articles written by her, one is given the impression that her concept of feminism may not entirely correspond to the conventional ideas of feminism. In an interview, she says:

> The women in my books are people who come to realize what it is to be a woman in the process of their own lives and the situations they face not through books and theories. I think feminism is an entirely personalized perception. It is when you start questioning preconceived notions about your roles. I don't think there is anything 'inherent' in a woman apart from the fact that she can conceive. All other things are equally important for them as they are for the men.[15]

There are no antagonists or villains in Deshpande's novels. She does not take sides with her characters, presenting them as close to reality as possible, portraying both their strengths and weaknesses. In her interview, she explains, "Once you understand the mind of a person you can't be harsh. I don't see in terms of black and white, all of us have several shades of grey in us." She further says that the men in her books are "never bad and the women never entirely good." The only unfairness she sees in the set up is the fact that "men, having made the rules of the game, have made the world a more comfortable place for themselves."

Many reviewers, however have interpreted the novel as a feminist critique written in the form of a novel. According to Toril Moi, "The principal objective of feminist criticism has always been political: it seeks to expose, not perpetuate, patriarchal practices."[16] This is what Shashi Deshpande does in *That Long Silence*. But as Sarla Palkar observes, "*That Long Silence* is also a self-critique. The important insight that Shashi Deshpande imparts to us through Jaya is that women should accept their own responsibility for what they are, see how much they have contributed to their own victimization, instead of putting the blame on everybody except themselves." (169) Jaya mostly blames herself for what she had been, she tells us that she is not writing a story of a callous, insensitive husband and a sensitive suffering wife. "I am writing of us," (1) she says.

It is, however, important to note that Deshpande's protagonist, Jaya, makes a powerful statement on the totally unfair system prevailing in our society. The most notable example is the family tree episode. Once Jaya's Ramu *Kaka* excitedly shows her the family tree he had prepared. He is very happy and proud of the fact that he had been able to go back nearly two hundred years to trace the line of their ancestors. Jaya, however, is shocked to find her name missing. Nor does the family tree include her mother, her aunts and most importantly her *Ajji* "who single-handedly kept the family together," (143) women who had married into this family. This amply illustrates the utter lack of importance for women in the Indian social set up. Another example of Jaya's anger and despair over the gross inequalities present in society is shown in her reaction to Manda's narration about her drunken father beating up her mother because she could not provide him with money to drink. Jaya begins to wonder:

> Where was it that I had read an account of how baby girls were done to death a century or so back? They were, I had read in horror, buried alive, crushed to death in the room

> they were born in, and immediately after that, a fire was lit on the spot—to purify the place, they said. Perhaps it was to ensure death. All those agonies—for days I had been unable to get it out of my mind. But now, I wondered whether it wasn't more merciful, that swift ending of the agony, once and for all, than this prolonging of it for years and years. (53)

At the end of the novel, Jaya very honestly questions herself: "But why am I making myself the heroine of this story? Why do I presume that the understanding is mine alone." (193) It is statements like this which prove that *That Long Silence* is not just another novel filled with hysterical ranting by a prejudiced writer but almost the diary of a sane housewife. Thus, unlike many other novels which are written from the feminist point of view, *That Long Silence* is "a muted and essentially sympathetic treatment of the problems of marital relationships; maintaining a credible balance between the sexes."[17] It has often been debated whether *That Long Silence* is a feminine novel or a feminist novel. However, Deshpande herself is not in favour of labelling her novels. She says:

> It is a curious fact that serious writing by women is invariably regarded as feminist writing—A woman who writes of women's experiences often brings in some aspects of those experiences that have angered her, roused her strong feelings. I don't see why this has to be labelled feminist fiction. A [male] critic once said about a novel of mine, "She can be quite brilliant when she is not raising her banners of protest." What banners of protest, was my thought. Any woman who writes fiction shows the world as it looks to her protagonist; if the protagonist is a woman, she shows the world as it looks to a woman—to apply the tag of feminist is one way, I have realized, of dismissing the serious concerns of the novel by labelling them, by calling the work propagandist.[18]

Taking the cue from the novelist, Keki Daruwalla, a distinguished Indian English poet, says: "Labels are inadequate here, as they always are when confronting a work of art. One cannot dub *That Long Silence* either as a feminist or psychological novel. It has been written by a strong personality, a fine craftswoman and a novelist with an unerring eye for character. Shashi Deshpande never over reaches herself."[19] We may, however, conclude that *That Long Silence* is both actual feminine writing and potential feminist writing, whether or not Deshpande is a formal feminist.

NOTES

1. Vimala Rama Rao, "Rev. of *That Long Silence*," *The Journal of Indian Writing in English*, Vol. 21, Jan. 1993, No. 1, 72.
2. Subhash Chandra, "Silent No More: A Study of *That Long Silence*," *Indian Women Novelists*, ed. R.K. Dhawan (New Delhi: Prestige, 1991), Set I, Vol. 1, 148.
3. Shashi Deshpande, *That Long Silence* (New Delhi: Penguin, 1989).
4. Adele King, "Shashi Deshpande: Portraits of an Indian Woman," *The New Indian Novel in English: A Study of the 1980s*, ed. Viney Kirpal (New Delhi: Allied, 1990), 166.
5. Sarla Palkar, "Breaking the Silence, Shashi Deshpande's *That Long Silence*," *Indian Women Novelists*, Set I, Vol. V, 166.
6. G.D. Barche, "Facets of Feminism," *Indian Women Novelists*, Set III, Vol. V, 15.
7. Alladi Uma, "Introduction: A Historical Background," *Woman and her Family, Indian and Afro-American: A Literary Perspective* (New Delhi: Sterling, 1989), 4.
8. Yasmin Ali Bhai, "No Sheltering Tree," Rev. of *That Long Silence*, *New Society*, No. 5, Feb. 1988.
9. Sudhir Kakar, *The Inner World: A Psychoanalytic Study of Childhood and Society in India* (New Delhi: Oxford University Press, 1981), 125.
10. Indira Bhatt, "*That Long Silence*: A Study," *Indian Women Novelists*, Set I, Vol. V, 156.

11. *Ibid.*, 157.
12. Purabi Panwar, "Breaking the Silence," Rev. of *That Long Silence*, *The Telegraph*, No. 4, Aug. 1989.
13. Sarla Palkar, 168.
14. Tapan Basu, "Joining a Select Club," Rev. of *That Long Silence*, *Sunday*, No. 8-14, May 1988, 98.
15. Shashi Deshpande, Interviewed by Malini Nair, "The Message is Incidental," *Times of India*, No. 25, Nov. 1989.
16. Toril Moi, *Sexual/Textual Politics: Feminist Literary Theory* (London: Methuen, 1985), 14.
17. K.C. Nambiar, "Eve in an Urban Jungle," Rev. of *That Long Silence*, *The Hindu*, No. 6, Mar. 1990.
18. Shashi Deshpande, "The Dilemma of a Woman Writer," *The Literary Criterion*, Vol. 20, No. 4, 1985.
19. Keki Daruwalla, "An Intense Book," Rev. of *That Long Silence*, *Indian Literature*, Vol. 34, No. 6, Nov.-Dec. 1991.

Coming to Terms With Tragedy: *The Binding Vine*

The day for moving mountains is coming.
You don't think so?
It is coming: for a while the mountain sleeps,
But in other times mountain all moved in fire.
If you do not believe that, Oh man, this at least believe:
All sleeping women will wake now and move.

Yosano Akiko, *The Day*

Desire, says the Buddha, is the cause of grief
But how escape th' cord
This Binding Vine of love?
Fear is coiled within this womb piercing joy.

The Binding Vine

The Binding Vine is a curious intermingling of three lives and is narrated by the sharp-tongued Urmi, a character drawn in almost the same vein as the protagonists of Deshpande's other novels. The weaving of three different tales into a single narrative is, in the main, due to the bereavement suffered by the narrator. Urmi is grieving over the death of her year old daughter Anu and in this condition she is highly sensitive to the suffering and despair of others. It is this sensitivity which leads her to befriend Shakuntala, the mother of a rape victim. Urmi would never have associated herself with Shakuntala in the normal course of her life as she belonged to a different strata of society altogether. It is the same sensitivity which also makes her delve into the poems of her long-dead mother-in-law, Mira and frantically try to understand the mind of the young Mira.

The novel opens with Urmila trying to cope with the death of her daughter and the efforts of her friend and sister-in-law, Vanaa, her brother Amrut and Inni, her mother to help her back to normalcy. Vanaa's pathetic attempts to remind Urmi of the great courage she had displayed in the incidents of their childhood are all dismissed by Urmi who feels that they are too petty to be compared to her grief now. She, in fact, wants to cling on to her grief and feels that she cannot betray her daughter's memory by trying to blot her out of her mind. Commenting on her masochistic attitude, S. Indira writes: "Instead of fighting her pain and sorrow, she holds on to it as she believes that to let go of that pain, to let it become a thing of the past would be a betrayal and would make her lose Anu completely. Like a masochist, she clings to her pain and allows her memories of Anu, every small incident to flood her with longing and a great sense of loss."[1]

It is in this state that Urmi meets Shakuntala, the mother of a rape-victim, Kalpana on her visit to a hospital where Vanaa works. Earlier the mother assumes that her daughter, who is now lying unconscious, has been injured in a car accident. On examination, the doctor informs her that she has been raped, in the process of which she is so badly injured that she is lying like a vegetable neither dead nor alive. The mother's reaction to this news is quite predictable. She tells Vanaa hysterically, "It's not true, you people are trying to blackmail my daughter's name."[2] Later on, catching a hint of the conversation between Vanaa and Dr. Bhaskar, the doctor in charge, she recoils in fear against the word, 'report.' She cries:

> "No, no, no. Tell him, tai, it's not true, don't tell anyone. I'll never be able to hold up my head again, who'll marry the girl, we're decent people, doctor," she turns to him, "don't tell the police." (58)

The narrator highlights her immediate concern here which is that the rape should remain a secret. In writing about rape, Deshpande has not attempted anything new but the way she has portrayed this sordid drama is very realistic. The characters spring to life and the anger, frustration, helplessness and despair of the victim's family are brought out evocatively. The narrator, Urmi, escorts the sobbing Shakutai to her house on Vanaa's request and from here begins their association. Urmi visits her regularly to inquire after her daughter and through their conversation we get a gleaning of Kalpana's life. While speaking of her daughter, Shakuntala is full of paradoxes. On one hand she says:

> She is very smart, that's how she got the job in the shop. Kalpana even learnt how to speak English. People in our chawl used to laugh at her but she didn't care. When she wants something, she goes after it, nothing can stop her. She's stubborn, you can't imagine how stubborn she is. (92)

A little later, she continues, however, pride giving way to resentment:

> And she's secretive. She never tells me anything. She didn't even tell me how much her pay was, can you imagine that? Me, her own mother. As if I was going to take her money away from her. I don't want anything. All I ask is that she help me out. (92)

On another occasion, Shakutai bursts out:

> She's very pretty, my Kalpana. She's not like me at all. When she was born, she was so delicate and fair, just like a doll, I wondered how a woman like me could have a daughter like that. (93)

The same Shakutai, however, condemns her for the very things for which she had praised her earlier:

> And I have to listen to such words because of this girl. She's shamed us, we can never wipe off this blot. And

> Prakash blames me—What could I do? She was so self-willed. Cover yourself decently, I kept telling her, men are like animals. But she went her way. You should have seen her walking out, head in the air caring for nobody. It's all her fault, Urmila, all her fault. (14)

Urmila, however, is unable to see the point in blaming Kalpana. She is outraged that the rapist will be allowed to get away scot-free, if the case is not registered as a rape. She tries to reason with Shakutai: "She was hurt, she was injured, wronged by a man; she didn't do anything wrong. Why can't you see that? Are you blind? It's not her fault, no, not her fault at all." (147) She is unable to convince Shakutai, who keeps saying, "But sometimes, I think the only thing that can help Kalpana now is death." (147) Shakutai who keeps meandering between praising her daughter and criticising or blaming her is "a victim of her own values. Yet she wasn't born with these values embedded within her mother's womb. Someone had to shape these values, make her believe that they were her own. Who? Her mother, her mother's mother, her mother's mother's mother? Not at all. It was her father, her father's father, her father's father's father, ad nauseam."[3]

The mother's reaction, no doubt, is a reflection of the society we live in, governed by age-old patriarchal norms. There is a strict code of conduct to be followed by girls regarding their dress, speech and behaviour in order not to attract the attention of men. A girl is advised at every step to avoid behaving like a male and to establish her feminine identity. A lot of importance is attached to the way she carries herself, the way she sits, stands, talks and interacts with others. Taking long strides denotes masculinity, and so a girl is told to walk with soft steps, so soft that they are barely audible to the others. It is considered sacrilege for a girl to dress or move in such a way so as to bring the contours of her body into greater prominence and attract people's attention.

If a girl is raped, then, according to the rules laid down by society, she is considered to be as much at fault as the rapist, if not more. Perhaps, there can be no greater injustice heaped on women than this. Worse still, the police whose duty it is to bring the culprit to book, prefer to record it as an accident as in the case of Kalpana. Dr. Bhaskar, the doctor in charge of the case, protests in outrage at the case being reported as an accident. Pointing out to the obvious signs of rape on the badly mauled Kalpana, he tells Urmi:

> "What about the injuries, I asked him? I'd examined the girl damn it," Bhaskar says angrily. "You could see the marks of his fingers on her arms where he had held her down. And there were huge contusions on her thighs—he must have pinned her down with his knees. And her lips bitten and chewed. Surely, I asked, no vehicle could have passed over her lips leaving teeth marks?" (8)

It is not as if the police officer needs to be convinced that it is a rape case. As he tells Dr. Bhaskar:

> She's going to die anyway, so what difference does it make whether on paper, she dies the victim of an accident or a rape. We don't like rape cases—They're messy and trouble-some, never straightforward. But forget that and think of the girl and her family. Do you think it will do them any good to have it known the girl was raped? She's unmarried, people are bound to talk, her name would be smeared. (88)

The police officer's argument, no doubt, aptly sums up the Indian psyche nurtured as it is in a culture which, in general, depicts women as grossly sensuous and licentious. So much so that in a crime as brutal as rape, it is the victim more than the accused who desires to remain anonymous. The ancient Hindu law-giver, Manu, whose philosophy occupies an important place in the Indian tradition and culture, is of the opinion of women that the creator "implanted in them carnal passions, love for ornament, impure desires, wrath, dishonesty, malice and bad conduct."[4] It is no wonder, then, as S. Indira observes: "Kalpana's mother Shakutai seemed to be more worried about the scandal which would certainly ruin the family's name and impair the marriage prospects of not only Kalpana but also her second daughter, Sandhya." (24)

Dr. Bhaskar finds it strange that women like Shakutai who have got nothing out of marriage except children, still live in fear of their children remaining unmarried. He is informed by Vanaa that Shakutai's husband had deserted her long ago for another woman and left her alone to fend for herself and the children. Hence he thinks it is a mystery that Shakutai should hanker after the marriage of her children when it had given her little comfort or happiness herself. As he tells Urmi: "Women are astonishing, I think it takes a hell of a lot of courage for a woman like that to even think of marriage." (87) Urmi replies that women marry in spite of everything because it provides security. She makes a valid point here and emphasises the vulnerability of single women in a social set up as ours, where men and women are expected to follow a rigid code of conduct keeping natural, biological feelings under control. The noted Indian English writer, Mulk Raj Anand, feels:

> No woman in our land is beyond the threat of rape, because of the suppressed energies of the male, through the taboos of patriarchy which deny sex before marriage and make male young into wanton animals who assault any possible victim when possessed by lust.[5]

It is, indeed, an irony that to avoid brutalisation of one kind, women willingly submit themselves to a brutality of another kind in the institution of marriage. Mulk Raj Anand agrees with Dr. Sudhir Kakar, a psychoanalyst, who mentions in his book that male chauvinism is more glaringly obvious in the lower level of society. Mulk Raj Anand says:

> In the slums men have no property except women, whom they can use for their ease, as unpaid slaves in the house, vehicles of lust and as victims from whom they can take

> out pain, to alleviate their own humiliation when insulted by their bosses. (33)

In spite of all her sympathies, Urmi is unable to do anything for Kalpana. She remains a mute spectator until the hospital authorities decide to shift her to a suburban hospital as beds are in much demand in the crowded hospital. Urmi then decides to take the matter to the press so that Kalpana may get justice. Urmi's crusade for Kalpana does not receive the approval of either Vanaa or Urmi's mother. Nevertheless, Urmi pursues the case. Eventually, the case is reopened and the identity of the rapist is revealed only in the end. However, a perpetuation of the tragedy cannot be avoided as the case draws to a close. The rapist is discovered to be Shakutai's sister Sulu's husband, who, it is later revealed, had always lusted after Kalpana. This revelation shatters Sulu who immolates herself in guilty despair, leaving behind her grief-stricken sister, Shakutai, who had adored her.

Deshpande encroaches upon yet another piece of hallowed ground, the almost entirely untouched subject of marital rape—hitherto considered a taboo subject by other Indian writers in English. She has written on the same subject in her novel, *The Dark Holds No Terrors*, in a different context. Here, the protagonist Sarita is assaulted at night by her husband, who vents his frustration on her as she becomes a successful doctor while he remains an underpaid lecturer. In *The Binding Vine*, however, Deshpande describes the obsession of a man with his wife and her intense dislike for physical intimacy with him, which finds voice in a series of poems discovered by the protagonist Urmi long after her death.

Many years after her marriage, Urmi is given an old trunk full of books and other odds and ends belonging to her long dead mother-in-law, Mira, by her husband's step-mother, who is referred to as *Akka*. *Akka* is also the mother of her friend, Vanaa. While handing over the trunk to her, *Akka* tells her how Urmi's father-in-law had been attracted to Mira, a college student, and how he had pursued and married her. Perusing the voluminous pile of writing left behind by the young Mira, Urmi fathoms the extent of forced sexual activity Mira was subjected to by her husband. The trunk is full of school note books which Mira had used as diaries, scribbling pads, untidy bundles of paper, a file and an envelope full of photographs. Reading through the cryptic poems and entries in her diary, Urmi is able to reconstruct the tragic tale of a sprightly girl who was condemned to suffer in an incompatible marriage. After a careful study she is able to decipher the essence of the thoughts which Mira had, perhaps, tried to put down on paper. From the book of poems presented to Mira by her father, it is evident to Urmi that her father was proud of her talent. Mira's photographs and writings resurrect in Urmi's mind an image of a vivacious and intelligent young girl. Her desire to be a poet and her inhibitions about expressing it aloud, her fear of being laughed at, are all obvious in her poems:

> Huddled in my cocoon, a somnolent silkworm.
> Will I emerge a beauteous being?
> Or will I, suffocating, cease to exist? (65)

Her innermost feelings find expression in her poems written in the vernacular, Kannada.

Mira, perhaps, symbolises the plight of countless women who face the same situation but are unable to voice their suffering. The invasion of one's body even though sanctified by marriage, can be as traumatic as rape. We come across a similar situation in Shashi Deshpande's short story "Intrusion" which describes the experiences of a honeymooning couple. It is a highly sensitive story where the husband imposes himself on his yet unprepared wife. These experiences evocatively bring out the humiliation experienced by the protagonist who feels her body has been violated by her crass and insensitive husband.

A husband imposing himself on his wife is, however, never publicised at least among the Indians where the Puranas dictate that it is a wife's duty to please her husband in bed. Tradition demands that a perfect wife should possess the following qualities:

Karyesi Dasi
Karyeshu Mantri
Roopecha Laxmi
Kshmaya Daridri
Bhuktesu Mata
Shayanesu Veshya
Shatkarna Yukta
Kuladharma Patni

Loosely translated, these lines mean that a wife should serve her husband like a slave, give him proper advice, look as beautiful as the goddess Laxmi, forgive all his sins however terrible they may be, feed him like a mother, and serve him like a prostitute in bed. These lines, often quoted as advice to wives, clearly show the injustice meted out to women who are expected to give top priority to their husband's pleasure.

It is no wonder, then, that Urmi's mother-in-law, Mira, had to put up in silence with the violation of her body. Her thoughts however, are recorded as poems for posterity. Urmi's careful translation of the Kannada poems into English reveals the pathetic condition of Mira. One poem particularly brings home her tragic despair:

But tell me friend,
did Laxmi too twist brocade tassels
round her finger and tremble,
fearing the coming of the dark-clouded engulfing night. (66)

Going through Mira's diary, Urmi is convinced that she had written from her personal experience. "She observes that it runs through all her writing a strong, clear thread of an intense dislike of the sexual act with her husband, a physical repulsion for the man she married." (63) To prove her point, Urmi narrates a passage where Mira had clearly put down on paper, the relationship she shared with her husband and her feelings or lack of them for him:

> Talk, he says to me, why don't you say something, why don't you speak to me? What shall I talk about, I ask him stupidly. "What did you do today, where did you go, what have you been thinking about all evening?" and so he goes on, dragging my day, my whole self out of me. But I have my defences; I give him the facts, nothing more, never my feelings. He knows what I'm doing and he gets angry with me. I don't mind his anger, it makes him leave me to myself, it is bliss when he does that. But he comes back, he is remorseful, repentant, he holds me close, he begins to babble. And so it begins. "Please," he says, "please, I Love You." And over and over again until he has done. "I Love You." Love: How I hate the word. If this is love, it is a terrible thing. I have learnt to say "no" at last, but it makes no difference, no difference at all. What is it he wants from me? I look at myself in the mirror and wonder, what is there in me? Why does it have to be me? Why does it have to be me? Why can't he leave me alone? (67)

Urmi is able to feel her pain and anguish years later and connects her sorrow to that of Shakutai's who also has the same thing to say, "Why does this have to happen to me?" (67) Urmi alleviates her grief by discovering and empathising with the sorrow of these women. Since the beginning of time, it had always been taken for granted that marriage provided a means for man to satisfy his sexual urge and to help in the task of procreation, and that woman was only a tool to be used towards that end. The feminist movement initiated in the West, shattered this myth and proclaimed that woman had every right to find fulfilment in the act of sex. Indian women, bred as they are in the culture which demanded their total subjugation however, could not even dream of asserting themselves in this aspect. While Deshpande's Mira represents women who are victims of marital rape, Anita Desai's Maya, in *Cry, the Peacock*, represents women whose husbands remain insensitive to their desires. Just as Mira silently subjects herself to the nightly assaults of her husband, Maya turns a psychological wreck unable to get any solace from her unresponsive husband.

Husbands and wives are thus bound in an institution which can hardly be called marriage. Simone de Beauvoir observes:

> Marriage is obscene in principle insofar as it transforms into rights and duties those mutual relations which should be founded on a spontaneous urge; it gives an instrumental and therefore degrading character to the two bodies in dooming them to know each other in their general aspects as bodies, not as persons.[6]

Going by this definition by Beauvoir, it would be no exaggeration to say that most Indian marriages are 'obscene,' conducted as they are, taking caste, creed, community, financial and social status and everything else except the feelings of the prospective bride and groom into consideration. Countless generations of women have been victims of loveless marriages and several generations will continue to be so in future if society chooses to ignore the feelings of women.

Though the novel, *The Binding Vine*, essentially revolves around the individual tragedies of Urmi, Mira and Kalpana, Deshpande hints at the raw deal faced by most women at different levels—whether it is women from chawls like Shakutai and Sulu, or the urban, educated women like Urmi's mother, Inni, her friend, Vanaa and her mother-in-law, *Akka*.

The Indian custom of changing the bride's name is a pivot point of transformation—a complete revamping of any young girl's psyche, so aptly documented in the saga of Deshpande's heroines or protagonists. Mira, who is bound in a marriage against her choice, cringes further when a new name 'Nirmala' is thrust on her. But she refuses to give up her name and proclaims:

> Nirmala, they call, I stand statue still.
> Do you build the new without razing the old?
> A tablet of rice, a pencil of gold
> Can they make me Nirmala? I am Mira. (101)

The degree to which Indian women are subjected to domination by their husbands is also evident from what Inni reveals to Urmi in reply to her unvoiced accusation against her parents for having left her to be brought up by her grandparents at Ranidurg. Inni pathetically confesses to Urmi that it was Urmi's father who had sent her away to Ranidurg as he did not trust his wife with looking after the child well as she had left the child in the lurch. Years later when she tries to explain to Urmi the reason why she was sent away, Inni pours out all the anguish of a woman who was helpless before the dictates of her husband. She says:

> Then he decided he would take you to his mother. He didn't say anything to me, he just took you away. I never imagined he wouldn't bring you back, I thought this was just to teach me a lesson, to punish me, but—I begged him, Urmi, I cried, I promised him I'd never leave you alone, but he wouldn't listen. Nothing could make him change his mind. You know your papa—I didn't want you to be sent away to Ranidurg, believe me Urmi, I didn't want that, I wanted you with us. I never got used to the idea of your being in Ranidurg, I wanted you with me. (200)

The level of submission practised by women in the interest of safeguarding their marriage is also hinted at in the glimpses offered into the marriage of Vanaa and Harish. Urmi, who is the more assertive of the two friends often reprimands Vanaa, whose constant refrain "Harish says," irritates her terribly. "Assert yourself," she tells her, "you don't have to crawl before him, do you?" (80) Urmi is also angry with Vanaa when the latter tells her wistfully of her secret longing to have a son which is ruthlessly denied to her by her husband. After the birth of their second child who is also a daughter, Vanaa tells Harish about her desire to have a son. But he quotes population figures to her and expresses surprise that she should be one of those women who crave for sons. And then, he also asks her why she should think for sure that the next child would be a son. In spite of all these arguments, Vanaa still feels that she would not have minded taking a chance. On hearing this, Urmi furiously bursts out, "You let him bulldoze you, you crawl before him." (81) She also admonishes Vanaa for trying to cope with her domestic duties single-handedly, and argues with her when she tries to speak on behalf of her husband:

> "Why can't Harish help?"
> "He comes home so tired . . ."
> "You know Vanaa, what you're going to become, coping with everything the way you are?"
> "What?"
> "A Super Woman."
> "Good! And doesn't that make Harish a Superman?"
> "No, a superbrat." (81)

Vanaa's daughter, Mandira, is a perfect example of how in general people grow up with pre-conceived notions of the role of a woman as a mother and wife. Mandira apparently thinks that a woman's first duty is to look after her home and children. She is resentful of the fact that her mother leaves her and her sister in the care of an *ayah*. This is evident from the way she declares to Urmi: "You know Urmi auntie, when I grow up, I'm never going to leave my children to go to work." (72) Urmi's attempts to reason with Mandira prove futile as she remains adamant on this issue repeating again: "I'll never leave my children alone." (72) One reads the recurring sagas of mothers over generations, enduring almost identical lifestyles. It is evident that the idea of the mother being solely responsible for taking care of the children has remained unchanged.

The marriage of *Akka* also proves how terribly unfair our society is towards women. She is made to marry a widower and the father of a child. Even before her marriage, she is warned that her prospective husband had been obsessed with his wife and after her death is now interested only in his son. In fact, he marries only so that his son can have a mother. Listening to *Akka* narrating the story to her and Vanaa, Urmi thinks: "The cruelty, the enormous cruelty of that silenced us." (47) This example, in a way, describes the fate of many women who stoically accept marriage under any condition, because marriage is the only goal in life for a girl in our society, and finding a groom the most difficult thing on earth. And so *Akka* willingly agrees to marry Kishore's father in spite of the risk of living under the shadow of a dead woman.

Deshpande also gives us a glimpse of women living at another level of society women like Shakutai and Sulu. Shakutai's husband leaves her in her father's home soon after their marriage so that he can search for livelihood in Bombay. When he does not return six months later, however, Shakutai joins him in Bombay, unable to stay any longer in her father's house. She realises that her husband is a lazy and good for nothing fellow who does not stick on to any job. They live in a relation's house where she is put through much humiliation. After the birth of three children one after the other, Shakutai takes it upon herself to work and support her family. In spite of doing all kinds of work to support her family, her husband deserts her for another woman. Shakutai does not hesitate to describe her husband as a useless fellow. Talking to Urmi of her unfulfilled desire to have a *mangalsutra* made in gold she says: "Then one day I thought—the man himself is so worthless, why should I bother to have this thing made in precious gold? That's been the greatest misfortune of my life, Urmila, marrying that man." (110) It is, indeed, tragic that in spite of putting up with such a worthless husband and in spite of struggling alone to fend for her children, fingers are pointed at her when anything goes wrong in the family as is the case when Kalpana is raped. As she tells Urmi, bitterly, in one of her conversations: "What can you expect, they say, of a girl whose mother has left her husband? Imagine! He left me for another woman, left me with these children to bring up." (147)

The condition of Shakutai's sister, Sulu, is no better either. From all accounts, she comes across as a very affectionate and sweet-natured person. She helps her sister in every way she can, and tries to take over the responsibility of bringing up Kalpana which is, however, thwarted by Kalpana herself. As we learn later, she is lusted after by Prabhakar, Sulu's husband. In her many talks with Urmi, Shakutai describes what a wonderful person her sister is and how well she kept her home, how beautifully she had decorated her sister's house for a *Haldi-Kumkum* ceremony and in general, what a marvellous person she is. All these attributes, unfortunately, do not find favour with her husband. As Shakutai tells Urmi: "After marriage she changed. She was frightened, always frightened. What if he doesn't like me, what if he throws me out? Nobody should live like that, Urmila, so full of fears. What kind of life is it?" (195) Deshpande shows how the institution of marriage can sometimes shatter the self-confidence of a person and transform a vivacious girl into a fearful and nervous woman.

The Binding Vine, with its assortment of women who seem to be victimised one way or the other, has prompted reviewers to present vastly contrasting opinions. In the words of Dermot Clinch: "*That Long Silence* was a gloomy novel but *The Binding Vine* is gloomier still."[7] In contrast, a woman reviewer, Shreya Cheravuri, feels that there is nothing in the novel to show blatant physical subjugation of women. She says: "The subjugation is not crude enough to be solely physical, though there is an example of that in Mira's marriage, but also intellectual, sexual and emotional. Still Deshpande does not fall into the trap of women-as-victims syndrome, which is an easy one to fall into in any feminist writing."[8]

In one of her interviews, Shashi Deshpande offers an explanation for this disparity in opinion between a male and a female reader. She says: "I find a lot of men unsympathetic to my writing and a lot of women extremely sympathetic. This is because the world is viewed in different ways by men and women. Women see a mirror image and men see, perhaps, a deformed image of themselves."[9]

In portraying the various women characters, Deshpande shows that they seek fulfilment only within the orbit of family and relationships. *The Binding Vine* explores important problems of our time without offering any facile solutions. Deshpande's characters may be independent to some extent but are firmly bound by the shackles of tradition. Urmila, perhaps, is the most rebellious of Deshpande's women characters. Unlike the protagonists in the other novels written by her, who are aware of the inequalities in society but do not attempt to set right anything, Urmila takes up cudgels on behalf of the rape victim, Kalpana. She is instrumental in publicising the case and getting the police to investigate the matter and find the culprit. She encourages her friend, Vanaa, to assert herself and stop behaving like a door mat. She also sets herself to the task of translating the poems written by her mother-in-law in Kannada to English and intends publishing them. All this has prompted Indira Nityanandam to write: "*The Binding Vine* is a refreshing change from the first three novels of Deshpande. Protest comes easily to her protagonist here and there is less agony in attempting to change societal roles and attitudes. The hope for Indian women lies in the happy fact that though there are Miras and Kalpanas and Shakutais, we also have our Urmilas."[10]

Urmila, nonetheless, does not display any radical attitude towards the institution of marriage. She argues with Dr. Bhaskar that marriage is a necessity and that for women like Shakutai marriage means security as it provides them safety from other men. Urmi herself remains totally faithful to her husband, Kishore, in spite of his long absences from home as he works for the Navy. Deshpande hints at a certain level of incompatibility in their marriage because of Kishore's withdrawn attitude. Reacting to Vanaa's advice that she should be more cautious in her relationship with Dr. Bhaskar, Urmi thinks:

> But how can Vanaa, secure in the fortress of her marriage to Harish, understand what it is like—marriage with a man who flits into my life a few months in a year and flits out again, leaving nothing of himself behind? Often, after he had gone, I find in myself a frantic grappling for his image, as if he has taken that away as well. (164)

During the long absences of her husband, Urmi confesses that there are moments when she is overcome with a longing for some physical gratification. Her friendship with Dr. Bhaskar provides ample opportunity to satisfy this urge as he declares that he has fallen in love with her. Urmi comes perilously close to responding to Bhaskar but holds back instead and thinks, "It's so much easier, so much simpler, to just think of virtue and chastity and being a good wife." (166) It is obvious to the reader that she will never overstep the boundaries chalked out in marriage. Deshpande leaves it unsaid, however, whether this virtue will ever be acknowledged by her husband. It goes without saying that men take their wives' loyalty for granted. Simone de Beauvoir rightly observes:

> A husband regards none of his wife's good qualities as particularly meritorious; they are implied by the institution of marriage itself; he fails to realise that his wife is no character from some pious and conventional treatise, but a real individual of flesh and blood; he takes for granted her fidelity to the strict regimen she assumes, not taking into account that she has temptations to vanquish, that she may yield to them, that in any case her patience, her chastity, her propriety, are difficult conquests; he is still more profoundly ignorant of her dreams, her fancies, her nostalgic yearnings, of the emotional climate in which she spends her days. (492)

The protagonist, Urmi, shows at every turn of the novel that she is fully aware of the unequal treatment meted out to women. She sympathises with Shakutai, encourages Vanaa to be more assertive and is totally absorbed by the writing left behind by her dead mother-in-law. In spite of all this, however, she does not consider marriage to be an obsolete institution. She may be educated and exposed to western ideas but nowhere does she show that she agrees with Simone de Beauvoir's famous statement: "It has been said that marriage diminishes man, which is often true; but almost always it annihilates women." (496)

Besides the main characters, Urmi, Vanaa, Mira and Kalpana, there are a few minor characters who merit our attention from the feminist viewpoint. There is Mira's mother who, going by Mira's account of her, could not think of a life of her own separated from the destinies of her children. Though Mira lived a generation before Urmi, she comes across as a person aware of her identity, and one who is aware that her potential goes beyond her assigned roles of mother and wife. This is evident from the writing in her diary:

> I remember the day the astrologer came home. He read all our horoscopes, told us our futures and we listened as if they were stories about other people. Only my mother's horoscope was not read. "Don't you want to know your future?" I asked her, she was serious when she said this—"What's there in my life apart from all of you? If I know all of you well and happy, I'm happy too." Did she really mean that? Will I become that way too, indifferent to my own life, thinking it nothing? I don't want to. I won't. I think so now, but maybe mother thought like me when she was my age. It frightens me. No, it doesn't, I'll never think my life, myself nothing, never. (101)

Deshpande also highlights the injustice meted out to women in the literary world where men dominate. This is not because women are not talented, but because men are considered creatively superior to women. Mira's diary reveals that Venu, a poet, whom she idolised, was contemptuous of her writing. When she gave him some poems of hers to read, he replied: "Why do you need to write poetry? It is enough for a young woman like you to give birth to children. That is your poetry. Leave the other poetry to us men." (127) Venu brings to mind the words of Ruskin as mentioned by Kate Millett in her book *Sexual Politics*:

> Ruskin is solicitous to warn women away from accomplishment. They may get a smattering of information, but they are given orders to halt at the point of difficulty: understanding the meaning, the inevitableness of natural laws and follow at least one of them as far as to the threshold of

> that bitter valley of humiliation, into which only the wisest and bravest of men can descend.[11]

However, not all Deshpande's male characters can be categorised as perpetrators of male dominance. There is Dr. Bhaskar who is very sympathetic to the problems faced by women. As the doctor in charge of Kalpana, he is very upset by the rape. He argues vehemently with the inspector who wants to report the case as an accident. He treats Urmi like an individual and not just as the wife of another man. He has a passion for justice and truth and predictably falls in love with Urmi who is committed to the same ideals. There is also Malcolm, a journalist, who was Urmi's classmate at one time. In his own way, he tries to contribute towards highlighting the prejudices in society. As Muriel Wasi observes: "Dr. Jain supplies an element of hope that there are men in India who feel as strongly as women do, on the brutal atmosphere of real and potential violence in which Indian women live. There are also journalists like Malcolm, who will make use of rape and other items of violence to keep the public conscience alive. They are not heroes, merely working journalists, but they serve a relevant purpose and stand for something positive and essentially humane."[12]

Deshpande, while propounding her own brand of feminism, nevertheless, does not desist from making a dig at pseudo-feminists like Priti, who in their over-enthusiasm to fight for equal rights for women, often end up with ideas which are never practical. In one of her conversations with Mira, where they are discussing a judgement in a case filed by a husband against his wife for restitution of conjugal rights, Priti is very excited that the judge had ruled that the wife could not be forced into a physical relationship with her husband against her will. Carried away by this judgement, Priti cries out excitedly: "Isn't it radical, absolutely earthshaking in this country I mean? Can you imagine the consequences?" (37)

Urmi who reacts more soberly reminds her that one judgement by a single judge, which can be appealed against and overruled, will not make any difference to all of womankind. She believes that laws cannot change women's lives and there are not many women who can go to court on such a matter. This discussion prompts Urmi to give her the example of Mira, and immediately Priti is convinced that she should make a film out of Mira's story. She requests Urmi to write the script which Urmi promptly refuses. Her reaction to Kalpana's story is also in total contrast to Urmi's. While Urmi is genuinely concerned about the injustice done to Kalpana, Priti seems to revel only in the sensational aspect of the incident as is evident from Urmi's narration:

> She goes on to talk of Kalpana, she's full of it, she gloats over the fact that an investigation has been ordered—"I think it's great that they could raise the issue in the Assembly, it just shows . . ." (185)

Priti's character is Deshpande's one attempt at satire which Shreya Cheravuri feels is not in keeping with her usual style. She writes: "The book shows flashes of irony as when the socially mobile do-gooder Priti, tries to adapt Mira's life into a film, and then takes on the cause of Shakuntala and her daughter Kalpana. But Deshpande's style is essentially too straightforward for satire and thus in parts, the book lacks a certain elegance."

The Binding Vine is a refreshing change from the earlier novels of Deshpande. According to Indira Nityanandam: "The step forward, achieved in this novel, is the introduction of female bonding, the desire of one woman to help another less fortunate one. Urmila draws society's attention to the plight of the rape victim and is determined to get Mira's poems published. This is a positive development in the protagonist, for Sarita, Jaya and Indu were involved in fighting only their own battles." (66)

Deshpande also takes a bold step forward in projecting a woman's biological needs and also raises the question of woman's right over her body which cannot be violated even in marriage. The novel can best be summed up in the words of Subhash K. Jha who writes in a review: "*The Binding Vine* is one of the few contemporary Indian novels to discuss its heroine's sexuality, her 'passion,' with a measure of unrepentant concern. In this novel Deshpande travels much further down the road in exploring the working women's needs of the head, heart and further down the anatomy, than her earlier novels."[13]

NOTES

1. S. Indira, "A Bond or Burden?: A Study of Shashi Deshpande's *The Binding Vine*," *Indian Women Novelists*, ed. R.K. Dhawan (New Delhi: Prestige, 1995), Set III, Vol. 6, 22.
2. Shashi Deshpande, *The Binding Vine* (New Delhi: Penguin India, 1992), 58.
3. Vikas Malik, "My Son You Rape Some Girls—But Marry a Nice Girl," Rev. of *The Binding Vine*, *Asian Times*, No. 29, June 1993, 9.
4. Quoted by Neena Arora, *Nayantara Sahgal and Doris Lessing: A Feminist Study in Comparison* (New Delhi: Prestige, 1991), 11.
5. Mulk Raj Anand, "In Yama's Hell," *Between Spaces of Silence—Women Creative Writers*, ed. Kamini Dinesh (New Delhi: Sterling, 1994), 33.
6. Simone De Beauvoir, *The Second Sex*, trans. H.M. Parshley (Harmondsworth: Penguin), 463.
7. Dermot Clinch, "Time for a Good Whine," Rev. of *The Binding Vine*, *The Independent*, No. 22, May 1993.
8. Shreya Cheravuri, "Caught in a Maelstorrn," Rev. of *The Binding Vine*.
9. Shashi Deshpande in an interview to Stanley Carvalho, "Everyone has a right to choose a language," *The Sunday Observer*, No. 11, Feb. 1990.
10. Indira Nityanandam, "Shashi Deshpande's *The Binding Vine*: *Silent No More*," *Indian Woman Novelists*, Set III, Vol. 4, 66.
11. Kate Millett, *Sexual Politics* (1969; London: Rupert Hart-Davis, 1971), 97.
12. Muriel Wasi, "The World of Women," Rev. of *The Binding Vine*, *The Financial Express*, No. 3, Oct. 1993, 9.
13. Subhash K. Jha, "Coming to Terms with Tragedy," Rev. of *The Binding Vine*, *The Economic Times*, No. 30, 1994.

"Marriage is not for everyone": *A Matter of Time*

> 'Maitreyi,' said Yagnavalkya, 'verily I am about to go forth from this state [of Householder].'
>
> *Brahad-Aranyaka Upanishad* (11.4.1)

Shashi Deshpande, who has carved a niche for herself in articulating the bitterness and desolation of her women characters in her novels, enters for the first time into a broader arena and grapples with the complex theme of alienation in her novel, *A Matter of Time* (1996). Also, for the first time in her career, Deshpande makes a man the protagonist of the novel. But, this does not mean that the novelist has totally shifted her focus. A close study of the novel reveals that Deshpande is deeply concerned as usual with the traumas suffered by women in a middle-class family in India. No doubt, the novel begins in a manner which is deceptively similar to her earlier novels and follows almost the same pattern, but there is something intrinsically different in its theme and presentation.

The novel revolves around an urban, middle-class family of Gopal. It begins with a crisis leading to an intense introspection by the protagonist. However, the first person narration which served to delve deep into the hearts of the women protagonists in Deshpande's earlier novels, for the first time successfully portrays the inner conflict in a man's mind, though it is sparingly used in parts of the novel. The author who has often provoked a debate about whether or not she is a feminist writer seeks, perhaps, to prove that she is capable of sympathizing with her male protagonists too.

In *A Matter of Time*, Deshpande gives an honest account of the abrupt disintegration of Gopal's happy family and the diverse reactions of all the people concerned. The passage from the *Upanishad* quoted above is a fitting epigraph to this novel which deals with a man's mid-life crisis leading to his desire for renunciation. Without any warning, Gopal one day announces to his wife that he is leaving the house for good. Sumi, his wife of twenty years, and their teenaged daughters, Aru, Charu and Seema are caught totally unawares. Sumi retreats into a shocked silence while eighteen-year-old Aru tries bitterly to search for her own reasons for this calamity.

Deshpande, who is an acknowledged master at expressing the anguish and frustrations of women, gives a true-to-life saga of the trauma faced by Sumi. The support of her immediate family—her parents, sister and cousins—comforts her to some extent, cushioning her against the cruelties of life. Unlike the general idea of a deserted wife, Sumi does not crumble to pieces at the pain and humiliation inflicted on her. As soon as she recovers from the shock, she picks up the threads of her life and tries to readjust her lifestyle to suit the situation. She moves with her children, into her parents' house and helps her children to get on with their lives as before. This monstrous tragedy, so undeserving as we are made to understand, leaves Sumi seemingly unperturbed. But beneath her apparent stoicism is a pathos left for the reader to decipher.

Sumi and Gopal's is not the ordinary arranged marriage. Gopal's frequent recapitulations allow the reader to share in their discovery of each other. Their joyous intimacy leaves one in no doubt of their compatibility—physical as well as mental. Recounting the rapture of their first physical union, Gopal thinks: "And I knew then that it was for this, this losing yourself in another human being, that men give up their dreams of freedom."[1] Their separation, therefore, is all the more poignant. Premi, Sumi's sister, is filled with a rage "at their carelessness in throwing away what they had, uncaring, it seems to her, of the value of what they have discarded." (136)

It is evident that there are no obvious reasons for Gopal walking out on his family. This is clearly established by the pathetic probing by Kalyani, Sumi's mother, who takes it upon herself to plead with her son-in-law to return home. Gopal reassures her that Sumi is not to be blamed for his decision, but does not offer any other convincing reason. Sumi's sister's attempt to elicit a reply from her brother-in-law also proves to be futile. On probing, Premi discovers from Aru and Charu that their father had been humiliated by his students in the college and had later resigned from his job. However, this does not seem to be a sufficiently concrete reason for his resolution. At times, it appears that even Gopal is not aware of the reasons for this momentous decision he has taken.

Vague references to his past by Gopal reveal that his childhood has not been normal. The fact that his father had married his brother's widow, and he was born of that union proves to be quite unsettling for Gopal. His adolescent mind draws up several possible reasons for this marriage. And, at one time, struggling with an inner conflict, he even draws a parallel from Hamlet's predicament:

> It was when I read *Hamlet*, fortunately much later, that the most terrible version of my parents' story entered my mind. Just that once, though, for I slammed the door on it immediately. In this story my father became a man succumbing to his passion for his brother's wife, the woman compliant, a pregnancy and a child to come and then after the husband's convenient death (no, I couldn't I just couldn't make my father poison his brother) a marriage of convenience. (43)

He is never able to relate to his father always thinking of him as his mother's guilty partner. Later, his parents' gruesome death leaves a void in his life. But, more than that, it is the realization, that his sister, Sudha, and he did not share the same father, that shatters his equilibrium. As he later reflects, "that was a betrayal that cut away at the foundations of my life." (52) It is obvious, therefore, that Gopal has long been nurturing a sense of loneliness and desolation as is evident from his ruminations:

no thought was given to the silent suffering and martyrdom of their wives. Lakshmana's steadfastness and devotion find no parallel in Indian mythology, while Siddhartha is hailed for spurning the luxury and comfort of princely life in pursuit of knowledge. Their respective spouses Urmila and Yashodhara, however, remain shadowy figures in the background, doomed to live a life of anonymity and insignificance. While Gopal is not idolized, he is not reproached either for shirking his responsibilities as a husband and father. On the other hand, Sumi is made to suffer the disapproving comments of women like Shankar's mother:

> "When are you going back to your husband?" the old woman asks abruptly. "You should be with him. Look at his state! It's all right to stay with your parents for a while, but that's not your home. When my daughters come home, I don't let them stay long. Go back to your husband, he's a good man. If you've done wrong, he'll forgive you. And if he has—women shouldn't have pride." (161)

Centuries may separate us from the mythical figures of yore, but even today a woman's worth is measured only through her marital status. This is graphically illustrated in the saga of the marriage of Sumi's parents, Kalyani and Shripati. Kalyani was an intelligent girl and was often playfully told by her father that she would become the country's first engineer. She was, however, not allowed to even complete her schooling and instead was married off to her maternal uncle, Shripati, according to her mother's wishes. Kalyani's mother, Manorama, is obsessed with the fear of her husband taking up another wife as she could not produce a male heir to their property and she does not even relish the idea of Kalyani marrying into a new family, as the property would then belong to them. Hence her desire that her only child, Kalyani, should marry her brother, Shripati. Such type of consanguineous marriages are quite common in South India where the main intention is to keep the property within the family. In spite of warnings from the medical fraternity about the risk of abnormalities in the products of such unions, these marriages continue to be contracted even to this day. Of Kalyani and Shripati's three children, the last one, who is a boy, is mentally retarded.

Tragedy strikes Kalyani when her four-year-old son gets lost in "that supremely Indian situation, confusion at a railway station"[4] as she is waiting to board the train to Bangalore. Shripati cannot forgive his wife for her negligence and sends her back to her parents's house with her two remaining children, Sumi and Premi. It is only on her death-bed that Manorama is able to prevail upon her brother to return and live in the 'big-house' with his wife and daughters. He obliges her but continues to maintain a stony silence with his wife. The enormous cruelty of it, apparently, does not cause as much concern as it would have, if, perhaps, Shripati had forsaken his wife or she had died. On hearing her grandparents's story, Aru is shocked at her grandmother's acceptance of such a life: "And when Kalyani signs her name, carefully, spelling out 'Kalyani bai Pandit,' Aru is amazed. How can she still have his name for god's sake?" (146) At times Sumi too wonders: "But for many others this may well be a sound arrangement where husband and wife are living together under the same roof even if there is only silence between them." Sumi recalls Shankar's mother's words "What is a woman without a husband?" (167) Sumi is unable to comprehend the meaning of such an existence. She thinks:

> Is it enough to have a husband, and never mind the fact that he has not looked at your face for years, never mind the fact that he has not spoken to you for decades? Does this wifehood make up for everything, for the deprivation of a man's love, for the feel of his body against yours, the warmth of his breath on your face, the touch of his lips on yours, his hands on your breasts? Kalyani lost all this (had she ever had them?) But her *Kumkum* is intact and she can move in the company of women with the pride of a wife. (167)

Deshpande in *A Matter of Time*, once again, touches on the aspect of female sexuality. Sumi recalls her friend, Vani, confiding in her when her husband was away for a year abroad, "oh, I miss him so much, . . . specially at night. There! it's out. I can't say this to anyone." (191) Sumi also looks at the mythical figure of Surpanakha from a new angle. She is unable to appreciate Rama and Lakshmana's treatment of Surpanakha:

> "She's as ugly as Surpanakha," she has heard Kalyani say. And she has been thinking since then of this demon sister of the demon king Ravana, who fell in love with the Aryan prince Rama. An unpleasant story, it's occurred to her, with the two princes Rama and Lakshmana mocking and ridiculing her and finally mutilating her by cutting off her nose. (191)

It makes her reflect:

> Female sexuality. We're ashamed of owning it, we can't speak of it, not even to our own selves. But Surpanakha was not, she spoke of her desires, she flaunted them. And therefore, were the men, unused to such women, frightened? Did they feel threatened by her? I think so. Surpanakha, neither ugly nor hideous, but a woman charged with sexuality, not frightened of displaying it. (191)

Through Sumi and Aru's eyes we are also made to witness the unfair treatment meted out to women in different spheres of life. Premi's story about one of her patients, the pregnant wife of an AIDS victim, shocks Sumi and Aru. The callousness of the man marrying, in spite of being aware of his condition, just so that he would have someone to look after him horrifies them and evokes their pity.

A chance remark by Nagaraj, a property dealer, about the ownership of the 'big-house' makes Sumi reflect for a moment on the injustice of her maternal grandfather's property being passed on to her father instead of her mother:

> Whose is it now? Baba's, yes, I know that. But it was

> amma's father's, it should have been hers. Why did they not give it to her? She finds herself looking into the conundrum of justice, a well so deep, dark and unfathomable, that she draws back. (196)

Aru is similarly surprised to learn from her lawyer/activist friend Surekha about the totally unfair system which had been in force in our country since time immemorial until recently. Aru, who plans to sue her father for maintenance, comes to Surekha for help. Surekha then tells her: "You're lucky to be living now. Do you know that Manu doesn't mention any duty to maintain a daughter? The duty is towards a wife, parents and sons." (204)

Aru also notices how the women in the family find no place in the family document held sacred by Kalyani. While the document is full of various characters and their descriptions, there is no mention of the women who undoubtedly had a hand in shaping the family tree. A similar observation is also made by Jaya in *That Long Silence* who protests against the family tree drawn up by her Ramu Kaka in which there is no trace of the women who have, according to her, played stellar roles in the family.

The deep-rooted desire of every Indian—male or female—to have a son is reiterated by Deshpande in this novel. Her quote from the *Upanishad* aptly sums up the Indian psyche:

> Whatever wrong has been done by him,
> his son frees him from it all;
> therefore he is called a son. By his son
> a father stands firm in this world.
>
> *Brahad-Aranyaka Upanishad* (1.5.17)

Kalyani is her mother's greatest disappointment in life. She was not an unloved child, but for Manorama, "she became the visible symbol of their failure to have a son." (151) Kalyani wins her mother's favour only once when she gives birth to a son. But this proves to be short-lived as she returns home in disgrace after the disappearance of this child.

In *A Matter of Time*, Deshpande, for the first time, writes from a man's point of view. From Gopal's introspection we get a clear idea of the insecurities and complexes of men. There is considerable hyperbole about the concept of motherhood and the feelings of a mother. But a father's feelings usually find no place, specially in the writing by women. Deshpande, however, gives a sparingly honest account of Gopal's emotions as a father:

> But I glimpsed it even then, the truth that would soon confront me, I saw it when Sumi put the baby to her breast. For I knew, when I looked at them, that they belonged together as I never did. Even when Sumi was impatient, when she showed a flash of temper as she often did for being deprived of her sleep, they were together in that magic circle. Woman and child. And I was outside. A man is always an outsider.
>
> I envied Sumi for this. And for this too: for a woman, from the moment she is pregnant, there is an overriding reason for living, a justification for life that is loudly and emphatically true. A man has to search for it, always and forever. (68)

The same feelings are reinforced by Gopal in response to Shankar who expresses his inability to protect his wife from his mother's sharp tongue saying, "She gave me birth, she brought me up, she looked after me." (216) Gopal understands his dilemma and observes:

> That's a debt we can never repay, it's a burden we can never lay down. Women will never understand this, they don't need to, they are luckier: the day they become mothers themselves, they have repaid their debt, they are unburdened and free. What is fatherhood set against this weight, this certainty of motherhood? (216)

Thus, Deshpande breaks herself free from the cordon she had earlier built around herself and successfully articulates the doubts and fears of her men characters with the effortless ease she had hitherto written about her women protagonists. In an interview, she expressed her desire "to reach a stage where I can write about human beings and not about men or women."[5] In *A Matter of Time*, she is able to achieve this to a great extent. She also proves, once again, that she is a writer incomparable when it comes to describing middle-class lives. In a recent review, Shama Futehally commends her for her realistic description and rightly observes: "Those who have read and reread Deshpande over the years are united in describing her as a 'middle-class' writer. In this they are paying her a great compliment; they are saying—with truth—that her writing is inseparable from the milieu she describes, or indeed from the readership she writes for. She writes as an insider, not as a viewer: that bane of post-independent writing which was so much more of a bane when Deshpande began her career." (111)

The novel ends on a tragic note with the sudden deaths of Sumi and her father, Shripati, in a road accident. This, perhaps, serves to justify the philosophical strain which runs through the novel. Gopal's answer to Premi's persistent probing underlines the inconsistency of life and the uselessness of living:

> You remember the Yaksha's question to Yudhishtira: What is the greatest wonder in the world? And what Yudhishtira's answer was? We see so many people die yet we go on living as if we are going to live forever. Yes, it's true, that is the greatest marvel the world holds, it's the miracle. In fact, it's the secret of life itself. We know it's all there, the pain and suffering, old age, loneliness and death, but we think, somehow we believe that it's not for us. The day we stop believing in this untruth, the day we face the truth that we are mortal, that this is our fate as well, it will become difficult, almost impossible to go on. And if that happens to all of us, the human race will become extinct. (134)

The passage, no doubt, gives "metaphysical probings into the world of the spirit,"[6] but the novel contains a lot else which the author tries to convey through the "idea of three women from three generations from the same family and how they respond to the tragedy that suddenly overpowers their lives."[7]

NOTES

1. Shashi Deshpande, *A Matter of Time* (New Delhi: Penguin, 1996), 223.
2. Hermann Hesse, *Siddhartha* (New Delhi: Rupa, 1993), Verso
3. Subhash K. Jha, "Knotty Problems," *Sunday*, Dec. 22-28, 1996, 54-55.
4. Shama Futehally, "Eloquent Silence," *The Hindu*, Jan. 19, 1997, 111.
5. Shashi Deshpande in an interview to Vanamala Vishwanath, "A Woman's World. . . . All the Way!," *Literature Alive*, Vol. 1, No. 3, Dec. 1987.
6. Sonia Trikha, "Metaphysical Meanderings," *The Express Magazine*, Oct. 27, 1996.
7. Subhash K. Jha, 55.

"Fractured Memories": *Small Remedies*

> Memory . . . carries its own truth with it. As long as there is memory there is always the possibility of retrieval, as long as there is memory, the loss is never total.
>
> *Small Remedies*

In her latest novel, *Small Remedies*, Shashi Deshpande seems to have honed her skills to perfection. Her protagonist is still the urban, middle-aged and educated woman, but her canvas has broadened to encompass a cross-section of people who belong to different communities, professions, and a level of society. Madhu Saptarishi, is not much different from her counterparts Indu, Sarita, Jaya, Urmi and Sumi in age, education and family background. Also, all of them in some measure or the other face upheavals in their marriages—upheavals which are inevitable when a woman refuses to conform to her accepted role as wife, mother or sister. But, moving away from her near perfect portrayal of a traditional Kannadiga-Maharashtrian Brahmin family, Deshpande ventures to write about a Goan Christian family and also mentions a Muslim *tabla* player and briefly touches upon his life and the people surrounding him, notably his grand-daughter, Hasina.

In a review, Meenakshi Mukherjee briefly sums up Deshpande's works and observes the noticeable change: "In *Small Remedies*, Deshpande is attempting much more than she did in her earlier novels—all five of them different from each other—but smaller than this in scope. . . . But none of them gathered up, as this new novel does, in one large sweep, the plurality, diversity and contradictions of our composite culture where an Anthony Gonsalves (the reference to "Amar Akbar Anthony" is deliberate), a Hamidabai and Joe can all be part of Madhu's extended family, and the daughter of Ghulam Saab can opt, though not very easily to get accepted as Shailaja Joshi."[1]

Yet another successful first attempt has been Deshpande's foray into the world of classical music. Madhu is writing the biography of a famous classical singer, Savitribai Indorekar, doyenne of the Gwalior Gharana, and this calls for a deep understanding of Hindustani music on the part of the author. Deshpande never falters and seems to be on familiar ground, using the jargon and idiom of music quite effortlessly and all the while writing in her impeccable English. As Meenakshi Mukherjee observes: "Of the four remarkable novels I have read in recent times that deal with music—Vikram Seth's *An Equal Music*, Salman Rushdie's *The Ground Beneath Her Feet*, Bani Babu's Bangla novel *Gandharvi* and now *Small Remedies*, Shashi Deshpande, I think, faces the toughest challenge. This has to do with incompatibility between the discourse of Hindustani music and the English language."

The novel, however, is less about music and more about the fascinating vocalist, Savitribai Indorekar. In spite of Deshpande's repeated denials of being a feminist writer, she creates characters who often contradict such statements. Savitribai is one such character, vividly portrayed and brought to life by the author. Physically she appears to be a frail woman. Looking back, Madhu remembers her as:

> a small sized woman. Even from my child's perspective she had seemed petite. Age and illness have so shrunk her that she's a doll-sized woman now. . . . The skin is fine and delicate, even if it is crinkled like tissue paper. Her arms are slim and firm, but the hands, with their branching of veins, seem incongruously large for those delicate arms.[2]

She is, however, imperious in her attitude to her servants, students, and even her biographer, often giving her instructions on how to conduct the interview. It needed tremendous grit and determination to be born in a traditional, orthodox Brahim family and make a name for oneself in the field of classical music. Madhu observes the unspoken resentment in Bai's voice when she recalls how she was abruptly asked by her grandmother to stop singing when she was performing as a child during a family gathering. Madhu herself recollects how "In Neemgaon she was 'the singer woman' and there was something derogatory about the words, yes, I can see that now, about the way they said them." (29)

But Madhu refuses to pander to the publisher's wishes to write a trendy feminist biography. They feel that "Victim stories are out of fashion, heroines are in." (167) Madhu, however, "cannot impose the new concept of heroinism on an old-fashioned woman who whitewashes her life through selective amnesia."[3] She records the life of a young woman who had lived a sheltered life of a daughter-in-law of an affluent Brahmin family, a woman who even as a child had been part of a large family. For a woman with such a background to elope with a Muslim *tabla* player and live in a strange town among total strangers must have required immense courage.

That there are different yardsticks for men and women in our society is obvious to Madhu who, in her childhood, was a witness to the rejection of Savitribai by conventional society. She remembers how in Neemgaon "each family had its place marked out for it according to religion, caste, money, family background, etc." (138)

She is aware that her father with his unorthodox ways was an oddity. Being a widower and bringing up a daughter on his own with only a male servant at home, observing no rituals or religious customs and openly indulging in a drink or two every evening, he obviously stood out in a conservative place like Neemgaon. But, looking back, Madhu realizes that while people were willing to overlook her father's eccentricities and his foibles they were not so generous when it came to accepting Savitribai. "Being a man he could getaway with much. He could live the way he wanted without open censure or disapproval." (139) It is only when a woman dares to defy convention that people are shocked. As Madhu observes, "In a sense, neither of us belonged. Munni's family, with her singer mother, absent father and another man—a muslim—sharing the home, was of course radically, shockingly different." (138)

Madhu also gives the example of Savitribai's father-in-law, who had a mistress, a singer famous for her Thumri singing. It was common knowledge that he visited her regularly. The women looked on in amusement and gossiped about it. They wondered at his choice of a mistress but there was never any outrage over the fact. "That he had a mistress was accepted, a wife from one's own class, a mistress from another—this was normal." (220)

For a man to indulge in his love of music and even to have a singer for a mistress was alright. But, for a daughter-in-law to be learning music seriously, as if she was going to be a professional, was scandalous and unthinkable. Though Bai had the support and encouragement of her father-in-law, Madhu could imagine the anger, contempt and ridicule she had to face from the other women when she returned to her life among the women, after her music classes. She could imagine the jibes and the hostility and the way she would have been cast aside like an untouchable. She says:

> To be set apart from your own kind, not to be able to conform, to flout the rules laid down, is to lay yourself open to cruelty. Animals know this, they do it more openly, their cruelty towards the deviant is never concealed. But the subtle cruelty of persistent hostility leaves deeper wounds. There's always the temptation to succumb, to go back to the normal path and be accepted. To resist the temptation speaks of great courage. (221)

Madhu also remembers the gossip surrounding Bai in Neemgaon. There was a Station Director who frequented Bai's house and got her many contracts with the radio, and was generally believed to be her lover. Madhu remembers the children teasing Munni and calling him her *mama*, a kind of euphemism for a mother's lover. Bai denies the existence of any lover, while recounting her story to Madhu. But to the town, in Madhu's childhood, it was very simple—why would a man go out of his way to do so many favours for a woman, why would he visit her so often? All such assumptions ending finally in the conclusion: "A woman who'd left her husband's home—what morals would she have, anyway!" (222)

Madhu is left quite confused at times about Bai's courage or lack of it. She had, undoubtedly, led the most unconventional life anyone in her society would ever imagine. But behind these acts of bravado was a woman who wanted to conform, to be accepted by society.

Savitribai was not the stereotypical feminist with a devil-may-care attitude. This is evident in her blanking out Ghulam Saab's name while relating a story of her life to Madhu, her biographer. This reveals her anxiety to cover up her youthful indiscretions in order to present a picture of respectability. She even goes to the extent of hiding the details of her daughter born through her association with Ghulam Saab. Madhu who is aware of Savitribai's past and her daughter Munni, is unable to digest her indifference to her daughter, more so, because Madhu herself is a doting mother, grieving over the death of her son.

Madhu feels that she can give Bai the immortality she desires only if she is willing to pay the price of revealing her daughter to the world—a daughter whose existences she had successfully obliterated until then. She cannot understand why, when she had the courage to walk out on her marriage and family, she was so frightened to reveal the existence of her child. She wonders how "She gave that child the name 'Indorekar'—the name she adopted as a singer—not comprising either her maiden name or her married one. Meenakshi Indorekar. Marking her out as *her* child alone, not the child of her marriage, not the child of her lover. This surely is a statement I cannot ignore?" (169)

Munni, however, desperately hankered after the name her mother had left behind and went to great lengths to dissociate herself from her father and, after a while, her mother, Bai had found conventional life stultifying, but Munni yearned for it all her life. As a child Madhu recollected how Munni refused to accept Ghulam Saab as her father and instead concocted stories about a lawyer father who lived in Pune. She also remembered how the girls in their neighbourhood tormented her with questions:

> What's your name?
> What's your father's name?
> Where is your father?
> Who's the man who lives with your mother? (77)

Years later when Madhu met Munni in a bus and recognised her, the latter refused to answer to the name of 'Munni' or even acknowledge her childhood friend. She declared that her name was 'Shailaja Joshi,' trying as it were, to desperately wipe out any connection with her past.

Deshpande, while writing of people like Savitribai and Leela, people who dared to be different, has also created characters like Munni who desperately seek the approval of society. Malathi Mathur, a reviewer, writes: "At the other end of the spectrum is Munni, Savitribai's daughter who turns her back on her mother and all that she stands for, in a desperate desire to conform, having encountered early in life the poisoned barbs that society levels against those who dare to be different."[4]

Apart from Savitribai, Madhu's narrative also includes the saga of another equally, or perhaps more, remarkable woman, her aunt Leela who was "ahead not only of her generation, but the next one as well." (94) She was a fiercely independent woman and was strongly committed to the communist ideology. She had participated in the Quit India Movement, but was critical of Gandhiji's principles of *Ahimsa* and *Satyagraha* and thought that it was ridiculous to allow oneself to be beaten up. As she grew older, however, she mellowed down and regretted some of her actions. It was evident that she was no run-of-the-mill activist, but a woman who had the courage of her convictions. She resigned from her party when she felt that the party's reaction to a political situation was not appropriate.

Though Leela was a generation older than Madhu, she was financially independent and supported herself. When her first husband, Vasanth, died she took up a job and educated her brothers-in-law. She lived in the crowded chawls among the cotton mills and worked for the welfare of the women afflicted with TB. It was this which first brought her into contact with her second husband, Joe, a doctor who had established a clinic especially for TB patients.

Leela and Joe were poles apart and Madhu exclaims at the strangeness of Joe falling madly in love with her. He was a widower with two children, spoke impeccable English and was very widely read, quoting from his favourite writers at the drop of a hat. Literature and music were the two great forces of his life, in addition to medicine. Leela, on the other hand, wore 'ayah saries,' according to Phillo, Joe's housekeeper. She spoke no English and knew nothing of literature or music. She had no sense of humour, according to Joe. But theirs was a wonderful companionship and a beautiful relationship, according to Madhu.

Leela was a person who disapproved of a life that did not look beyond one's own self. Madhu recollects her reaction to the film 'Devdas.' When she remained silent for a long time after watching the film, Madhu thought that the film had evoked memories of her dead husband, who like the hero of the film had died of TB. But what Leela had to say surprised and amused Madhu, Joe and Tony: "Now I know," she said, as if she had solved a puzzle. "Now I know why that poor man drank so much. He had nothing to do, he didn't have any work at all. . . . If an intelligent man like him remains idle, what else can he do but take to drink?" (96)

Leela disliked the superior status her family gave itself and wondered what made them so special. She did not find anything even remotely worthy in their holding on to the lands which they had inherited. She did not believe in the caste system and was the only one among Madhu's relatives who accepted Madhu's parents' marriage and invited them to stay with her when they had no place of their own.

Leela was a passionate believer in the communist ideology

but did not hesitate to speak up against the party when the need arose. After putting in years of hard work, she was sidelined by the party bosses and never reached the top of the hierarchy, while men who worked under her reached there easily enough. Once, a widow of a sitting member, who was killed, was given a ticket to stand for elections. This provoked Leela, who had never earlier complained, to comment, "It seems you've got to become a widow for them to remember that you exist." (224) This is, indeed, a telling statement on the chauvinism that rules all political parties.

Savitribai too understood how much more difficult it was for women to rise to the top when compared to men. Madhu wondered if she had ever heard the phrase 'gender discrimination,' but she had certainly experienced and accepted it as the normal course of things. Madhu remembers how she had once commented caustically speaking of a young instrumentalist who had reached the pinnacle in no time: "Now a days they become *Ustads* and *Pundits* even before they have proper moustaches." (224)

At the foreground of the novel is the story of the narrator Madhu herself. She is commissioned to write the biography of Savitribai. She had always been intrigued, even as a child by Bai's relationship with Ghulam Saab and Munni, their daughter. The novel covers that period of her life when she is grieving over the death of her only child, Aditya. In remembering and re-telling the stories of Leela, Savitribai and Munni, she presents the glaring inequalities in gender in society. The pity of it is that some of the victims are not even aware of the injustices heaped on them.

Madhu herself is a victim of sorts of which the reader is aware only towards the end of the novel. She had been brought up as a child by two men—her father and Babu, a male servant, but she had no complaints. On the other hand, she felt pity for the children who seemed to be constantly harrassed by their mothers. She says:

> Motherless child that I am, motherhood is an unknown world to me. The mothers I see in my childhood are drab

> creatures, forever working, forever scolding their children, certainly they are not the women to arouse a sense of deprivation in me. (182)

Deshpande spares no effort to present the picture of life it is without conforming to stereotypes. This is all the more obvious in her portrayal of motherhood, which she seldom glorifies. Her protagonist, Madhu, says:

> I get some images of motherhood in the movies I see myself through the songs that speak of '*ma ka pyar.*' But real life shows me something entirely different. Munni's mother who ignored her daughter; Ketaki's mother, stern, dictatorial and so partial to her sons; Sunanda, sweetly devious and manipulating. Som's mother, so demanding—none of them conform to the white-clad, sacrificing, sobbing mother of the movies. (183)

But Madhu herself, turned out to be a doting mother and ever perceptive of her son's every need Therefore it was all the more tragic when Aditya, her son, died in a bomb blast.

Madhu's estrangement with her husband, Som, began earlier than this tragedy, when Madhu, waking up after a nightmare, one night, revealed to him a secret which she had locked up in the innermost recesses of her mind. She had slept with a man when she was only fifteen, a man who later committed suicide. Som is unable to accept this of his wife. As one who had been a good husband by any standards and shared a wonderful relationship with his wife, he is now unable to come to terms with this news. He is totally devastated. Madhu is unable to comprehend this:

> But it's the single act of sex that Som holds on to, it's this fact that he can't let go of, as if it's been welded into his palm. Purity, chastity, an intact hymen—these are the things Som is thinking of, these are the truths that matter. (262)

It does not matter that Som himself had a full-fledged relationship with another woman before his marriage. It is a typical situation where a man may have any number of affairs but expects his wife to be a virgin. It's all the more undigestible to Som that his wife had been a willing partner. Madhu thinks "that he could, perhaps, have borne: that I had been raped, forced into the act, that I was a victim, not a participant." (260)

Our society has been so conditioned as to categorize women as immoral on the slightest deviation on their part from the normal course of behaviour. Madhu observed how Hari and Lata looked at her when she returned after inadvertently spending a night in a hotel room with Chandru. She thinks:

> It does not matter that Chandru is Som's friend and Chandru and I had been friends as well for nearly 25 years. I remember the waiter's look last night, when he brought us our dinner, the gleam in his eyes when they rested on me.
>
> Men and women can never be friends. Men can be brothers, fathers, lovers, husbands, but never friends—is that how it is? (254)

Shashi Deshpande has repeatedly expressed her displeasure at being considered the champion of oppressed women. It is, indeed, a tribute to her that some of the reviewers recognise her for what she is. Malati Mathur writes: "In portraying struggles of these women for identity, Shashi Deshpande waves no feminist banners, launches into no rabid diatribes. She drives her point home with great subtlety and delicacy."

NOTES

1. Meenakshi Mukherjee, "On her own terms," *The Hindu*, 7th May 2000.
2. Shashi Deshpande, *Small Remedies* (New Delhi: Viking, Penguin India, 2000), p. 14.
3. Meenakshi Mukherjee, *The Hindu*, 7 May 2000.
4. Malati Mathur, "Rebels in the household," *India Today*, April 3, 2000.

Technique and Style

It is widely accepted that "the novel is the readiest and most acceptable way of embodying experiences and ideas in the context of our time."[1] The manner in which to write a good novel, however, remains highly debatable. Many modern critics believe that in the past too much attention was paid to the story or plot overlooking psychological aspects. Some modern novelists have written novels that are experimental and far removed from the traditional story-telling methods. According to Somerset Maugham, these writers who are dubbed anti-novelists, "consider the telling of a story for its own sake as a debased form of fiction."[2] The principal features of the anti-novelist, according to Paul Verghese, are "lack of an obvious plot; diffused episode; minimal development of character; detailed surface analysis of objects; repetitions; experiments with vocabulary, punctuation and syntax, variations of time sequence, alternative endings and beginnings."[3]

The narrative technique employed by the novelist is also gaining importance, considering the gradual increase in the different methods of story telling. Plain narrative or story telling is still the most common method employed by the novelist who is omnipresent and omniscient in this type of writing. The first person narrative is usually employed by the novelist to make his story appear more realistic and more credible. While novels written in such a manner have a ring of authenticity to them, they do not enable the novelist to look deep into the minds and motives of the rest of the characters. Shashi Deshpande overcomes this problem by using a combination of the first person and third person narrative coupled with flashback devices to lend force and realism to the novel. A chronological analysis of Deshpande's development as a novelist requires a keen study of the narrative techniques employed by her, beginning with her first full length novel, *Roots and Shadows*. The novel essentially deals with the protagonist Indu's painful self-analysis. The author also tries to encompass several other themes in this slim novel. Apart from the obvious and central theme of Indu's relentless probing to discover herself, there is the theme of bohemianism in the person of Naren in stark contrast to the middle-class values of Indu's family. There is the theme of woman's fate in general which is brought to the reader's notice, unobtrusively, in the form of Indu's observations. There is also the theme of the old order giving way to the new—symbolised by the demolition of the old house to construct a hotel. As Shama Futehally observes: "this slender novel attempts, in a way, to encompass too many themes, and is unable to develop them beyond making reflections on each which are almost in the nature of asides."[4] Other critics like Madhu Singh, however, are highly appreciative of her skill in interweaving myriad themes into a coherent whole. Comparing *Roots and Shadows* with *That Long Silence*, Madhu Singh points out that the former "is the more powerful of the two. In its succinctness lies its strength and the punch."[5]

To capture the interest of the reader, Deshpande avoids the simple technique of straightforward narration, and instead employs the flashback method. While the first chapter deals with the present, the later chapters move backwards in time, culminating in the final chapter which again ends in the present. This convoluted narration has come in for some criticism by reviewers who feel that it has only contributed to creating confusion in the minds of readers. For instance, Shama Futehally comments: "This is a device which is useful either when some element of suspense is needed, or for a novel with a non-narrative structure. For this novel chronological clarity is essential, as the reader already has to cope with an abundance of characters and their complex interactions. The first chapter, where we are faced with all of them simultaneously, and without introduction, is rather confusing." The entire novel is written in the first person, the narrator being a young woman writer who returns to her childhood home and finds herself caught in the whirlpool of family intrigues. Seen through the eyes of a young woman with liberated and progressive ideas, ordinary everyday incidents acquire a new meaning and highlight the gross inequalities in society. The first person narration also allows the author to probe deep into the mind of the protagonist, exposing her fears and frustrations with admirable candour, inviting the praise of reviewers like C.W. Watson, who compares Deshpande to the master story teller, Chekhov: "Other South Indian writers have been compared to Chekhov, but Shashi Deshpande, in this novel at least, comes closest to that writer, and the tragi-comedy of *The Cherry Orchard* is constantly recalled in the description of the crumbling house and the squabbling of the family. The writing is beautifully controlled and avoids the temptation of sentimentality which the subject might suggest and again the control is reminiscent of Chekhov."[6]

The Dark Holds No Terrors is commendable for its honest portrayal of the psychological problems faced by the protagonist, Sarita, a career woman, achieves a rare level of authenticity because of the use of a double perspective—the shifting of the narrative from the first person to the third person in every alternate chapter. When asked by Lakshmi Holmstrom in an interview as to how she had hit upon this technique, Deshpande replied:

> The present is in the third person and the past is in the first person. I was doing it throughout in the first. But that's often a perspective I use in my short stories. I wanted to be more objective. So then I tried it in the third. But it wouldn't work at all. Yet I really needed to distance myself from the narrative in the present, otherwise it was going to be far too intense. And then I read an American novel by Lisa Alther where she uses this method. And the minute I came across her novel I thought—let me admit it freely—Oh god, this is how I am going to do my novel.[7]

This is how the novelist manages to tell the story objectively, and at the same time, "No summary will do justice to the intricate web the author has woven through the superimposition of the past over the present, through dreams, nightmares, flashback, introspection and simple staightforward third person narration."[8]

The Sahitya Akademi Award winning *That Long Silence* is a complex novel of despair and triumph, of suppression and freedom, all played out for the better part in the heroine's mind through memories and recollections. The narrative with its slow unknotting of memories and unravelling of the soul reads like an interior monologue quite similar to the stream of consciousness technique employed by the likes of Virginia Woolf. A particularly bad patch in the narrator's life makes her bring alive her past through ruminations. Prema Nandakumar, however, maintains that the novel "is not a forbidding stream of consciousness probe in the Virginia Woolf tradition. It is very much a conventional tale full of social realism evoked by links of memory. Not misty recollection but clear-eyed story telling."[9] The narrator achieves a kind of catharsis by an objective analysis of what went wrong with her marriage and why she had failed as a writer. According to the reviewer Rita Joshi: "The method is reminiscent of Samuel Beckett in plays such as *That Time* where the character sits centre stage while three voices go over his past."[10] The technique is, perhaps, best described by the narrator Jaya herself, who is telling her own story: "All this I've written—it's like one of those multicoloured patchwork quilts the *Kakis* made for any new baby in the family. So many bits and pieces—a crazy conglomeration of sizes, shapes and colours put together."[11]

The Binding Vine differs in its mode of narration from her earlier novels. The narrative structure in *Roots and Shadows, The Dark Holds No Terrors* and *That Long Silence* does not progress chronologically, but instead moves back and forth thematically, gradually relating one incident after the other until the entire story is revealed. In *The Binding Vine*, however, individual plots of three different stories are interwoven bringing together three women separated by age, status and education. The entire story is narrated in the first person by Urmi. To offer deep and intimate glimpses into the life of the narrator's mother-in-law, Mira, Deshpande uses the poetry and writing in her diary and note books. Urmi is able to brilliantly recreate the story of Mira—her unspoken anguish and outrage at being subjected to rape within marriage.

Small Remedies, Deshpande's most recent novel, works at different levels—the personal, the worldly, women's rights, communal violence, motherhood etc. It vacillates between the present and the past, delving into the lives of Savitribai, Leela, Munni, and the narrator Madhu herself. It is structured as a biography within a biography, with the writer, Madhu, often in a dilemma about how to tell her story. She wonders if a biography is an exercise in truth telling, and if it is, whose version must it be?

In all her novels. Deshpande seeks to faithfully reflect life as it almost is without resorting to any personal commentary and explanation. Her novels, dealing as they do with women's oppression, are highly susceptible to feminist harangue. But, it is a rare achievement that she has not fallen a prey to this temptation. Unlike Mulk Raj Anand, who takes pleasuree in being called a propagandist, Deshpande protests against her work being labelled 'propaganda.' She vehemently denies any attempt on her part to moralise as is evident from what she says in an interview to Sue Dickman: "Somebody once asked me if I have a social purpose in my writing and I very loudly said 'No,' I have no social purpose, I write because it comes to me."[12]

In another interview to Stanley Carvalho, she once again emphatically states: "I hate to write propagandist literature. I think good literature and propaganda do not go together. Any literature written with some viewpoint of proving something rarely turns out to be good literature. Literature comes very spontaneously and when I write I am concerned with people."[13] She takes pains to explain that her writing merely mirrors the world. She finds that a lot of men are unsympathetic to her writing while a lot of women are sympathetic. The reason for this, according to her, is not difficult to analyse because in her writing, "women see a mirror image and men see, perhaps, a deformed image of themselves."[14]

But, as she matured as a writer, Shashi Deshpande has undergone a change of outlook regarding the scope of committed writing in literature. This is made clear when she candidly admits:

> There was a time when I was scornful of what is called committed writing. I considered such writing flawed because its being message-oriented diminishes its artistic worth. But now I know that all good writing is socially committed writing, it comes out of a concern for the human predicament. I believe, as Camus says, that the greatness of an artist is measured by the balance the writer maintains between the values of creation and the values of humanity.

It must be observed that Deshpande makes a sparing use of irony, satire or even humour which are the ingredients of great works of art. Flashes of irony are evident in one or two incidents in a couple of novels but they do not seem to be included intentionally by the writer. The most obvious example which comes to mind is the scene in *That Long Silence* where Mohan, Jaya's husband, accuses her of avoiding him during the crucial period when they are in hiding because of the fear of corruption charges being levelled at him. It is during this period that Jaya herself is facing a traumatic time and needs support. Her husband's accusation, therefore, seems highly ironical and throws her off balance for sometime. She keeps telling herself:

> I must not laugh, I must not laugh . . . even in the midst of my rising hysteria, a warning bell sounded loud and clear. I had to control myself, I had to cork in this laughter. But it was too late. I could not hold it any longer. Laughter burst out of me, spilled over, and Mohan stared at me in horror as I rocked helplessly. (122)

She is able to regain her sanity only after she decides to break her silence and record her story.

Another example of Deshpande's attempt at irony is her creation of the character, Priti, in *The Binding Vine*. Priti who at best can be called a psuedo-feminist provides a foil to the ever serious Urmi. Urmi's compassion for her long dead mother-in-law, Mira, makes her want to set Mira's random writings to order and publish them. But Priti is more interested in the sensation which Mira's story is likely to create and plans to adapt her life into a film. Her reaction to Kalpana's tragedy also borders on hypocrisy because she is more concerned about the publicity which the case is sure to generate. The reviewer Shreya Cheravuri, however, feels that Deshpande's novels could do without such devices because, as she says, "Deshpande's style is essentially too straightforward for satire and thus in parts, the book lacks a certain elegance."[16]

Deshpande also, by her own admission, steers clear of sentiment and romance. Speaking at a seminar, she expresses her annoyance at not being taken seriously by publishers. One publisher happened to reject her story and advised her to send it to a woman's magazine instead. This irked her and she began to wonder: "Why did the editor say that? It was a good story. I knew that. I was pretty confident about it. It was not a sentimental, romantic love story either, the kind that would fit smugly into a woman's magazine."[17] Deshpande probably feels that romance, sentimentality, and other such features merely diminish the serious concerns of a novel.

The use of myth is also recognised as an important literary device to enhance the artistic effect of the novel. While English poets and writers have relied heavily on Christian, pagan and classical myths, Indian writers in English have derived inspiration from the wealth of material available in the form of stories from the *Ramayana*, the *Mahabharata* and the *Puranas* and also local legends and folk-lore. The most often used symbol from Indian mythology, of course, is Sita, who is considered to be the ideal woman—patient and submissive. Many other parallels are also drawn liberally from Indian mythology by indian writers in English and other languages.

In *The Dark Holds No Terrors*, Deshpande draws a parallel from the Dhruva story to highlight the sense of neglect experienced by Saru, whose parents show a blatant preference for her brother, Dhruva. Saru's father also tells her how on her death-bed her mother had made him repeat the episode of Duryodhana's hiding in the lake at the end of the battle, waiting for the Pandavas to come and kill him. Saru identifies herself and her mother as Duryodhana figures—both lonely, unloved, defeated and filled with a sense of rejection.

In *That Long Silence*, Jaya recollects the fable of the foolish crow and the wise sparrow which she had often heard as a child. She does not repeat the story to her children because of the fear that they might store it in their subconscious and eventually turn out to be like "that damnably, insufferably, priggish sparrow looking after their homes, their babies . . . and to hell with the world. Stay at home, look after your babies, keep out the rest of the world, and you're safe." (17) Deshpande hints at the way in which the seemingly harmless bedtime stories influence children at a tender age to believe that a woman's job at all times is to protect her family even if she has to resort to treachery or deceit.

In *That Long Silence*, Jaya also recalls the *pativratas*—Sita, Savitri and Draupadi—mythical symbols of ideal wifehood, ironically comparing herself to them. "Sita following her husband into exile, Savitri dogging death to declaim her husband, Draupadi stoically sharing her husband's travails." (11) She feels that she has unconsciously emulated their example by following her husband into hiding when he is faced with the threat of corruption charges. There are quite a few mythical allusions in Deshpande's novels but she does not believe that myth is used as a literary device. In reply to Lakshmi Holmstrom's question if myth is a kind of language she uses, Deshpande says: "I think so. I think a number of us do that in India all the time; we relate a great deal of our personal lives, our daily lives, to the myths We find parallels as a matter of course. And we do this with all the myths, any myth that seems appropriate, whether they were originally about men or women. In that sense it is a part of a language, a grammar that one knows and understands, rather than a conscious literary device."

Narrative techniques apart, the most obvious challenge for the Indian writer in English is the use of English language in a way that will be distinctively Indian, and yet remain English.

Though Indian writing in English has come to stay, the propriety of Indian writers using English is still debated upon. Raja Rao in his 'Preface' to *Kanthapura* declares: "We cannot write like the English. We should not." The problem of the Indian English novelist is, indeed, unique. He or she writes in English about people who do not normally speak or think in English. In order to overcome this problem, novelists have made different experiments with language. According to Meenakshi Mukherjee, these experiments can be classified under three heads, "experiment in diction (literal translation of idioms), experiments in syntax (changing the structure of sentences) and imagery."[18]

Literal translation has been most consciously tried by Mulk Raj Anand who has no inhibitions of taking liberties with the English language in spite of the disapproval of reviewers and critics. Literal translations of Hindi and Punjabi phrases like "Are you talking true talk?" or "to make one's sleep illegal," are generously spread across his stories. Meenakshi Mukherjee in her book, *The Twice-Born Fiction*, has made a list of some of the Punjabi and Hindi idioms used by Anand in his works, some of which may sound atrocious to those not familiar with either of these languages. For example, 'eating the air' (to take a stroll), 'breaking the vessel' (to expose a secret), and 'black in the pulse' (something wrong). Anand's works are also liberally sprinkled with swear words and words of abuse, which of course are not out of place in stories mostly about the Punjab peasantry.

Khushwant Singh also translates many Punjabi phrases and proverbs into English. Bhabani Bhattacharya's novels are full of literal translations of Bengali proverbs, while Raja Rao's novels are full of translations of Kannada sayings. R.K. Narayan, perhaps, is the only one among the older generation who did not feel the need to use either any Indian translations of words and phrases nor original English text-book phrases. Among the later novelists, Anita Desai, Nayantara Sahgal and Kamala Markandaya have managed to use the English language without distorting it with unseemly translations of words and phrases or coining of new compound words like 'that-house-people' or 'next-house-woman's kitchen.' Shashi Deshpande belongs to the new breed of English writers who suffer from no complexes about using English because most of them do not even consider it a foreign language. According to Meenakshi Mukherjee: "Earlier English was the language of public discourse, of higher education. It is only for a section of those born in the 1950s and after that English is a first language, sometimes their only language. They display a careless intimacy with English, which enables them to play with it."[19]

Deshpande's writing is unplanned and quite spontaneous. Replying to Vanamala Vishwanath's observation that her writing is not obviously Indian and does not draw attention to itself, Deshpande replies:

> No, I don't believe in making it obviously Indian. But all this is basically because I'm isolated—I'm not part of any movement and not conscious of readers to impress. To get wider recognition here and abroad, you have to be in the university and places like that with the right contacts. I'm an ordinary woman who writes sitting at home. None of these things are within my reach. This has, I believe, done me good. It has given me great freedom. I'm happy with this anonymity. Once you get publicity-conscious, your writing becomes affected. I'm truly happy with this freedom.[20]

Deshpande, however, feels that writing in English in this country is a drawback because it alienates the writer from the mainstream. She seems to solve this problem by considering English, not a foreign language, but one of the Indian languages. She says:

> I believe that English writing in this country is a part of our literatures; I consider English as one more of our *bhashas* as Ganesh Devy calls them. I know that our writing comes out of an involvement with this society, out of our experiences here, our readership is now here, and happily our publishers are here as well. Yet, I am disturbed by

> the recent trend in English writing which in its pursuits of role models outside, is alienating itself from its roots.[21]

She feels that by writing in English she belongs to a small circle like the regional language writers and therefore, does not feel that it makes her non-Indian in any way. She does not approve of being categorised as Indian-English. She says: "I am an Indian writer. My language just happens to be English, which cannot be called a foreign language at all because it is so much used in India."[22]

Deshpande also very categorically rejects the use of Indian translations in her works to provide an Indian flavour, which was considered so essential by most of the earlier writers. She says:

> I do not use Indianisms to make my writing look Indian. I never try to make India look exotic. I do not think of a western audience at all. I belong to Indian literature. I would not like ever to be called an Indo-Anglian writer. I feel strongly about that.[23]

Deshpande feels that she is different from other Indians who write in English because she was never educated abroad and so her background is firmly rooted here. Emphasising this, she says:

> My novels do not have any westerners, for example. They are first about Indian people and the complexities of our lives. Our inner lives and our outer lives and the reconciliation between them. My English is as we use it. I don't make it easier for anyone really. If I make any changes, it's because the novel needs it, not because the reader needs it.[24]

Shashi Deshpande is aware of the problem faced by the Indian writers in English but feels that writers should work out their own language. She expresses happiness with the present breed of Indian writers in English whose writing seems to be aimed at Indian readers more than western. She is also happy that the present day writers seem to have got away from the obsessions with East-West conflict which has little relevance today. Deshpande, however, admits to failure at times to express the right emotion in a language alien to the characters she creates. She says: "I lose the range of nuances which are available in Marathi, for example, the richness of the phrases that make up that language."[25]

Deshpande's mind is ever alert to the issues related to contemporary society, and she has evolved literary skill in a manner which enables her to present these issues realisticaliy. Small wonder if the *Times Literary Supplement* showered praise on her creative use of language: "Deshpande eschews linguistic pyrotechnics and formal experimentation, but has sufficient command of her tradition to give the lie to the belief that the English language is incapable of expressing any Indian world other than a cosmopolitan one."[26]

NOTES

1. R.K. Dhawan, "Preface," *Explorations in Modern English Fiction* (New Delhi: Bahri, 1992), 1.
2. Somerset Maugham, quoted by Paul Verghese, *Literary Criticism—A Work Book* (Madras: Macmillan India, 1981), 80.
3. *Ibid.*, 80.
4. Shama Futehally, "Outgrown Flaws," Rev. of *Roots and Shadows*, *The Book Review*, March-April, 1984.
5. Madhu Singh, "Intimate and Soul Searching Portrayals of Marriage," Rev. of *Roots and Shadows*, *Indian Book Chronicle*, Vol. 18, No. 7, July 6, 1993, 22.
6. C.W. Watson, "Some Recent Writings from India," Rev. of *Roots and Shadows*, *Wasafiri*, Spr. 1995, No.21. 75.
7. "Interview: Shashi Deshpande talks to Lakshmi Holmstrom," *Wasafiri*, Spr. 1993, No. 17, 23-24.
8. Meenakshi Mukherjee, "Ghosts from the Past," Rev. of *The Dark Holds No Terrors*, *The Book Review*, Vol. 5, No. 5. Mar.-Apr. 1981, 31.
9. Prema Nandakumar, "Every Woman in Bombay," Rev. of *That*

Long Silence.

10. Rita Joshi, "Something Felt," Rev. of *That Long Silence, Hindustan Times*, No. 6, May 1990.
11. Shashi Deshpande, *That Long Silence* (New Delhi: Penguin India, 1989), 188.
12. "In Conversation: Sue Dickman with Indian Writers," *The Book Review*, Vol. 19, No. 4, Apr. 1995, 34.
13. Shashi Deshpande in an interview to Stanley Carvalho, "Everyone has a Right to Choose a Language," *The Sunday Observer*, No. 11, Feb. 1990.
14. *Ibid.*
15. Shashi Deshpande, "Of Concerns, Of Anxieties," *Indian Literature*, Vol. XXXIX, No. 5, Sept.-Oct., 1996.
16. Shreya Cheravuri, "Caught in a Maelstrom," Rev. of *The Binding Vine.*
17. Shashi Deshpande, "The Dilemma of a Woman Writer," *The Literary Criterion*, Vol. 20, No. 4, 1985, 35.
18. Meenakshi Mukherjee, "The Problem of Style," *The Twice-Born Fiction* (New Delhi: Arnold Heinemann, 1971), 170.
19. Meenakshi Mukherjee quoted in "An Area of Brightness," *The Week*, 26 July 1996, 14.
20. Shashi Deshpande in an interview to Vanamala Vishwanath, "A Woman's World . . . All the Way!" *Literature Alive*, Vol. 1, No. 3, Dec. 1987, 11.
21. Shashi Deshpande, "Of Concerns, Of Anxieties," 108.
22. Shashi Deshpande interviewed by M.D. Riti, "There's No Looking Back for Shashi Deshpande," *Eve's Weekly*, June 18-24, 1988, 28.
23. *Ibid*, 28.
24. Lakshmi Holmstrom, *Wasafiri*, 26.
25. *Ibid.* 24.
26. Maria Couto, "In Divided Times," Rev. of *That Long Silence, Times Literary Supplement*, 1 April 1983.

Conclusion

A close study of Shashi Deshpande's novels reveals her enormous sympathy for women and their travails, provoking reviewers to assume that she has joined the band of feminist writers who have achieved much popularity in the west. She, however, does not approve of being labelled a feminist writer. Though Deshpande refuses to be called a feminist writer, her novels are susceptible to a feminist approach. She has a remarkable insight into the working of a woman's mind. As a writer, she highlights the secondary position occupied by women and their degradation which is inevitable in an oppressively male-dominated society. She gives us a peep into the state and condition of the present-day woman who is intelligent and articulate, aware of her capabilities, but thwarted under the weight of male chauvinism.

Deshpande's women are the products of a painful period of transition in society where they have a greater share of responsibilities than their predecessors. They also have a number of avenues open before them and, in many fields, they have also proved themselves better than their male counterparts. In spite of their remarkable achievements, the general attitude towards women has not changed correspondingly. In the institution of marriage, the age-old rules with regard to the accepted behaviour of husband and wife remains almost unchanged, despite an overt display of Western influence.

Shashi Deshpande's novels are concerned with a woman's search for her identity—an exploration into the female psyche Her protagonists undergo an arduous journey to discover themselves and this leads them through a maze of self-doubts and fears. In her novels, she depicts woman in myriad roles—wife, mother, daughter and an individual in her own right.

In all Deshpande's novels, except *Come Up and Be Dead,* the protagonists are married women. Hence her depiction of woman as wife requires special mention. According to Rani Dharkar, "the importance that our society attaches to marriage is reflected in our literature. It is the central concern of Deshpande whose heroines, caught in the quagmire of marriage, struggle to come up for air."[1] Marriage is, perhaps, the most complex of human relationships. It is defined as a "cultural phenomenon which sanctions a more or less permanent union between partners conferring legitimacy on their offspring."[2] Marriage is not simply a social institution. It is inextricably linked to religion, and religion, being a potent force in our country, determines more or less the code of conduct in marital relationships. Almost all the religions of the world give sanction to female subjugation by the male members of society, thereby perpetuating the myth of female servitude. The Bible categorically tells the woman:

> Wives, submit yourselves to your husbands as to the Lord.[3]

The ancient Hindu law-giver, Manu, whose philosophy occupies a prominent place in the mainstream of Hindu ideology and culture, proclaims: "Even though the husband be of bad character and seeks pleasure elsewhere he must be constantly worshipped as a god by a faithful wife."[4] Thus, it is clear that since time immemorial woman has been given an inferior position in society. It is also obvious that woman has been defined most exclusively in her role as wife. This view is substantiated by Susan Wadby who, in her essay, "Women and the Hindu Tradition," says: "The dominant norms for the Hindu woman concern her role as wife. Classical Hindu laws focus almost exclusively on this aspect of the woman. Role models and norms for mothers, daughters, sisters etc., are less prominent and are more apt to appear in folklore and vernacular tradition."[5]

Shashi Deshpande succinctly presents the inequalities and injustice heaped on woman because of her subordinate status. In *Roots and Shadows*, through the eyes of Indu, the protagonist, we are made aware of the plight of various women like her

Kakis and Atyas. The heart-rending account of Akka's child marriage reveals the appalling condition of women barely a couple of generations ago. The inferior position of a wife in any marriage is made obvious through glimpses into the marriages of Indu's numerous aunts and uncles. It is clear that Indu, who, is proud of her liberated outlook, falls a prey to age-old tradition and unreasonable convention. Deshpande also exposes the sham and hypocrisy prevalent in the so-called urban, educated men like Jayant who are ostensibly influenced by the West and who pretend to possess progressive ideas, but are, in reality, as chauvinistic and fettered to time-worn conventions as their less educated and exposed counterparts. He belongs to a society which prides itself on its sophistication and refinement, but at home he remains a conventional husband expecting his wife to play a very submissive role.

Saru's husband, Manohar, in *That Long Silence*, is a glaring example of men with fragile egos, who find it difficult to accept the superior status of their wives in society. Deshpande also holds society responsible for the disastrous condition of Saru's marriage. Manu, who already suffers from an inferiority complex, is further humiliated by the cruel remarks of his colleague's wife and those of the girl who interviews Saru.

Mohan, Jaya's husband in *That Long Silence,* is a typical Indian husband who takes his wife's unflinching support for granted. When threatened with charges of corruption, he expects his wife to follow him into hiding without a murmur of protest. He does not mind using his wife as a crutch in his hour of crisis and the slightest hint of deviation from her role of a subservient wife is enough to provoke a terrifying outburst with which he walks out of the home. Deshpande also shows how Jaya herself is to be blamed for the state of her marriage. In retrospection, Jaya realizes how she had all along followed her Vanita mami's advice that a husband is like a 'sheltering tree' which must be kept alive at any cost because without the tree the wife becomes dangerously unprotected and vulnerable. Jaya thinks that she has "to keep the tree alive and flourishing even if you have to water it with deceit and lies."[6]

In *The Binding Vine*, Deshpande makes a bold attempt to tackle the subject of marital rape. Through the character of Mira, she focuses attention on all those women who are doomed to silently suffer nightly assaults by their husbands because the very idea of a woman protesting against her husband's sexual advances is unheard of in our society. Deshpande also hints at the lack of compatibility in Urmi's marriage even though hers is a love marriage. Through the character of Shakutai, Deshpande shows how at the lower level of society, marital vows are flouted most casually by men like Shakutai's husband. He is a good-for-nothing drunkard who leaves his wife and three children to fend for themselves and hankers after another woman.

The monogamous nature of women is hinted at in almost all the works of Deshpande. In most of her stories, the protagonist shares a greater level of compatability with a man other than her husband. This compatability often leads towards crossing of the boundary of platonic friendship and progresses towards physical attraction. But Deshpande's women do not overstep the limits of propriety except in the case of Indu in *Roots and Shadows* who resorts to an extra-marital relationship with Naren in an attempt to assert herself.

In *The Dark Holds No Terrors*, Saru meets her former classmate Padmakar Rao and the renewal of their friendship seems to border on an affair. Padmakar Rao who reveals a dissatisfaction with his wife tries to lure Saru into a relationship. Vulnerable though she is, with the horrifying nocturnal attacks by her husband, Saru refuses to accept the advances made by him. She is however not averse to being flaunted around by Boozie who, she is aware, is using her as a cover to his homosexuality.

In *That Long Silence*, Jaya finds a perfect match in Kamat, a widower who lives in a flat above hers. He is well-read, and apparently he is a good critic. So he is able to offer her constructive criticism with regard to her writing. She is perfectly at ease in his company and confides all her problems in him. She is never made to suffer any condescension in his company and this sets him apart from all the other men she has known in her life. In course of time, their friendship progresses towards physical attraction, but Jaya controls herself and ruthlessly suppresses her desires, in spite of the ample opportunity provided in the seclusion of his apartment. Safeguarding her marriage is of such paramount interest to Jaya that on finding Kamat dead in his flat one day, she prefers to remain silent for the fear of getting involved in a scandal, thereby jeopardizing her marriage.

Similarly, Urmi's association with Dr. Bhaskar in *The Binding Vine* develops into more than a platonic relationship. Urmi, whose husband is a naval officer and away for many months in a year, yearns at times for physical gratification. Dr. Bhaskar's self-admitted interest in her and her own attraction towards him offer her an opportunity to indulge in a physical union. But she refuses to let herself be enticed into an extra-marital affair.

Another recurrent relationship in Deshpande's novels is that between a mother and a daughter. Love and devotion to the mother is an integral part of the Indian psyche. Mythologies and literatures down the ages have always glorified the mother figure. Much has also been written about a mother's selfless love for her children. But the preference for a son is as old as Indian society itself. A wife's worth shoots up if she gives birth to a boy. Vedic verses pray that sons should be followed by more sons, never daughters. For example, a prayer in the *Atharvaveda* reads:

> The birth of a girl grant it elsewhere, here grant a son.

There are, of course, economic and religious reasons behind such an attitude. The presence of a son is absolutely necessary to perform many rituals, the most important ones being those that are carried out upon the death of the parents and which are considered imperative for the well-being of their souls. The daughter, therefore, has not only a negligible ritual significance but is also considered an enormous financial burden inasmuch as she does not contribute to the family income and instead takes away a considerable part of her family fortune as dowry.

But despite the yearning of all mothers to have sons, a mother's love for her daughter cannot be denied. Sudhir Kakar in an article on "Feminine Identity in India" says that "the special maternal affection reserved for daughters, contrary to expectations derived from social and cultural prescriptions, is partly to be explained by the fact that another's unconscious identification with her daughter is normally stronger than with her son."[7] Shashi Deshpande's protagonists, however, never seem to be on cordial terms with their mothers. In *Roots and Shadows*, Indu's mother dies in childbirth and so there is no delineation of the mother-daughter relationship. In *The Dark Holds No Terrors*, however, this relationship has a significant place. The entire novel, in fact, revolves around Saru's relationship with her mother. It is Saru's antagonism towards her mother and her rejection of the age-old traditional values represented by her that drive Saru into the arms of Manohar. During the crucial years of puberty, Saru develops an aversion to all traditional practices because of her mother's cold and indifferent attitude. She studies medicine to displease her mother and later marries out of caste to defy her. Even on her death-bed, Saru's mother has only curses for her daughter. Saru, in turn, does not record any warm feelings of her daughter in her recollections, though she makes sure to provide her daughter with all the material comforts and luxuries that she herself had been denied.

In *That Long Silence*, though there is no overt display of hostility between Jaya and her mother, it is evident that they do not share the same level of cordiality as Jaya and her father. Like Saru, Jaya too agrees to marry Mohan at the slightest hint of disapproval from her mother, and like her again she does not seem to have any strong maternal feelings towards her daughter. In a couple of instances, however, Jaya displays a stronger attachment towards her son. This provokes Subhash K. Jha to comment, "being intellectually equipped to scrutinize male prejudice, she [Jaya] still reveals an unmistakable partiality towards her son. The daughter is a mere blur in the narration, while the son (the heir apparent, the procreator) is described in glowing terms."[8]

In *The Binding Vine* too, it is obvious that there is no compatibility between the sophisticated Inni and her daughter, Urmi, the protagonist. At one point, in a choked and guilt-laden voice,

Inni bursts out that Urmi had been sent to Ranidurg as a child to be brought up by her grandparents, because Urmi's father did not approve of the way his wife was bringing up the child. Shakutai also shares a love-hate relationship with her daughter, Kalpana. She keeps vacillating between praising her daughter and blaming her for the catastrophe.

These illustrations reveal that the relationship between mother and daughter in Deshpande's fiction is far from being warm-hearted. Adele King rightly comments: "in all Deshpande's works there is no mother who could serve as a model for the daughter."[9] In an interview to Vanamala Vishwanath, Deshpande admits that she does not believe in painting a rosy picture of motherhood. She says:

> It is necessary for women to live within relationships. But if the rules are rigidly laid that as a wife or mother you do this and no further, then one becomes unhappy. This is what I have tried to convey in my writing what I don't agree with is the idealization of motherhood—the false and sentimental notes that accompany it.[10]

Deshpande, therefore, rejects the stereotyped image of mother and refuses to use any mawkishly sentimental language to describe the mother-child relationship.

A study of Deshpande's novels from a feminist viewpoint also reveals the essential loneliness of the heroines bordering on alienation, reminding us of the plight of the protagonists of Anita Desai. In *The Dark Holds No Terrors* where Saru as a child grows up almost resenting her mother, while her father remains a shadowy figure in the background. The man she falls in love with and marries, eventually turns out to be a psychological wreck with whom she cannot have a meaningful relationship. Her guru, Boozie, turns out to be a homosexual who had been merely using her as a pawn to hide his sexual preferences. Padmakar has his own selfish reasons for wanting to develop a more intimate relationship with her. He likes to meet her because he finds no companionship in his wife who cannot think beyond mundane needs of everyday life. In her disillusionment, Saru thinks, "Love . . . how she scorned the word now. There was no such thing between man and woman. There was only a need which both fought against futilely, the very futility turning into the thing they called love."[11] Saru's own children are described as quite indifferent to mother, and Saru herself does not indulge in any sentimental feelings towards them. Social visits to their friends' homes are described as routine and uninteresting and friends, both Saru's and Manu's, provide no comfort either. At times the novel reads like an existentialist tract devoid of any sentiments and underlining the loneliness of man.

In *That Long Silence* too, Jaya stands alone in her hour of crisis. It is evident that after seventeen years of marriage, Jaya's relationship with Mohan goes no deeper than physical attachment. Her relationship with the other members of her family remain superficial and she seems to derive no satisfaction even from her children. The only person who offers her a satisfying companionship and who animates her dies abruptly, leaving a void in her life. Even the physical attraction she initially feels for her husband gradually dwindles into routine and mechanical affair, making her feel that "love is a myth without which sex with the same person for a lifetime would be unbearable." (97)

In Deshpande's sixth novel, *A Matter of Time*, the theme of alienation is even more pronounced. The author quotes extensively from the *Upanishads* to explain the sense of rootlessness and desolation experienced by the protagonist, Gopal, who abandons his wife and three teenaged daughters for some strange and inexplicable reason. The author also describes the pain and humiliation of Sumi, his wife, who copes with the situation admirably and tries to provide emotional and financial security for her three daughters.

Deshpande's latest novel, *Small Remedies*, is "a book about writing a book" with reflections on the impossibility of ever capturing in words the truth about any life. It examines, in retrieving memory, the complexities in encapsulating the life of Savitribai Indorekar, who is devoted to music. Running through the narrative of this remarkable woman is the saga of Leela, who defies conventional norms and remarries after her widowhood. It is through Madhu's eyes that we get to know the dark corners of Bai's life and the illuminating saga of Leela. In portraying the struggles of these women for identity, no overt postures of feminism are struck.

Shashi Deshpande's frank and uninhibited discussion on a wide range of topics concerning women has prompted several reviewers to categorize her as a feminist. A close study of her work also reveals that she is a highly sensitive writer who is clearly aware of the male-female imbalance in society. Her male characters conform to the standard feminist description of a middle-class husband who is insensitive, egoistic and sometimes over-ambitious. But, at the same time, most of her women characters too suffer from some weakness or other so much so that it becomes difficult to label her work.

The term feminism itself demands a broader definition. In a generic way it has come to mean a movement to support the demand for equal social, political and economic rights with men. Feminism connotes not only an awareness of women's plight but also a determination to change the situation. The treatise 'Half the Sky' aptly defines feminism as "the awareness of the women's position in society as one of disadvantages or inequality compared with that of men and also a desire to remove those disadvantages."[12] One wonders whether Deshpande as a novelist fulfills these two requirements so as to be termed a feminist writer. We may not be sure of her strong desire to remove the disadvantages of women in society, but even a casual reading of her novels and short stories convinces us that they abound in her acute awareness of women's disadvantages and unequal position in society. In a recently published article, she writes:

> Most of my writing comes out of my own intense and long suppressed feelings about what it is to be a woman in our society, it comes out of the experience of the difficulty of playing roles enjoined on me by society, it comes out of the knowledge that I am something more and something different from the sum total of these roles. My writing

> comes out of my consciousness of the conflict between my idea of myself as a human being and the idea that society has of me as a woman. All this makes my writing very clearly woman's writing.[13]

Deshpande's novels bear out and even demonstrate what she holds in theory. *Roots and Shadows* is mainly concerned with women who are given a raw deal. Beginning with the protagonist Indu, the novel is replete with the private agonies of several women covering a wide cross section—educated women, illiterate women, widows, child-brides, domestic servants—all of whom have some genuine grouse or other. *The Dark Holds No Terrors* is a typical example of a husband's inability to come to terms with his wife's superior social and economic status. Deshpande gives a vivid portrayal of a woman who falls a prey to her husband's frustrations when he realizes that she has overtaken him professionally. The novel also traces the traumatic childhood of Saru who is the victim of gender bias at the hands of an insensitive mother.

That Long Silence is an autobiographical account of Jaya, a gifted writer, whose talent lies smothered under the disapproval of her husband. Jaya seeks to erase the long silence by giving an honest and frank account of the conditions which lead to her failure as a writer and the constraints of society which result in the suppression of her self as an individual.

The Binding Vine is a tragic tale of rape sanctioned by marriage in the case of Mira and the brutal rape of Kalpana. It reveals the trauma involved in a rape whether committed within or outside the precincts of marriage. The novel, in a subtle way, also traces the martyrdom of women like Inni, Vanaa and Shakutai.

Thus, the novels of Shashi Deshpande clearly reveal the author's perception of the endemic imbalance between the sexes. It is, however, obvious that the author stops short of trying to correct this imbalance. The numerous minor characters in the novels suffer in silence or accept their fate with resignation but do not take any step which might jeopardize their marriage or reputation in society. It is however important to note that each of her novels ends on a note of determination by its protagonist who resolves to take the reins of her life into her hands. Indu in *Roots and Shadows* emerges in greater control over herself at the end of the novel. She puts Akka's money to use according to the dictates of her conscience and does not bow to pressure from any quarter. She also gives up the job, where she had earlier worked only to avoid displeasing her husband, and settles down to pursue her writing, something which she had always wanted to do. With her new found sense of liberation also comes the realization that any freedom she devises must be within the boundaries of her obligations and responsibilities. She is able to appreciate what Naren's father says about rules adding grace and dignity to life.

Saru in *The Dark Holds No Terrors* is finally liberated and she is no longer afraid of the dark. Kamini Dinesh's observation aptly sums up Saru's development as an individual in her own right, "To be true to herself, the woman has to excoriate the film of superimposed attitudes and roles. Her emancipation is not in repudiating the claims of her family, but in drawing upon the untapped inner reserves of strength."[14] At the end of the novel, Saru stands poised to receive her husband secure in her new found confidence in herself. She successfully rids herself of her complexes and guilts and comprehends the meaning of human life where she realizes that she is not the only one facing the predicament of loneliness: "Alright, so I'm alone. But so's every one else. Human beings . . . they're going to fail you. But because there is just us, because there's no one else, we have to go on trying. If we can't believe in ourselves, we're sunk." (220)

That Long Silence too ends on a note of hope, with the protagonist Jaya's realization that she is no less to be blamed for allowing herself to be dictated by her husband and by the conventions of society. She achieves a kind of catharsis by penning her story and she is able to view the situation more objectively. She says: "I'm Mohan's wife I thought, and cut off bits of me that had refused to be Mohan's wife. Now I know that kind of a fragmentation is not possible." (191) This awareness helps her to cast aside the role she had willingly played all her life.

The Binding Vine is, perhaps, the only novel where the heroine, Urmi, is less wrapped in her own discontentment and, despite her recent bereavement, or because of it, gets involved in the misfortunes of others. She shows a positive attitude towards the victims around her. She resolves to get Mira's poems published and is determined to draw society's attention to the predicament of the rape victim, Kalpana. Indira Nityanandam observes that "the step forward achieved in this novel, is the introduction of female bonding, the desire of one woman to help another less fortunate one."[15] Comparing *The Binding Vine* with Deshpande's earlier novels, Nityanandam comments: "*The Binding Vine* is a refreshing change from the first three novels of Shashi Deshpande. Protest comes easily to her protagonist here and there is less agony in attempting to change societal roles and attitudes." (66)

What, however, we have to bear in mind is that Shashi Deshpande does not take the radical view of the early Western feminists like Simone de Beauvoir, Germaine Greer and Kate Millett. The opinion of most of these feminists with regard to marriage remains more or less the same. In her famous book, *The Second Sex*, de Beauvoir writes: "It has been said that marriage diminishes man, which is often true, but almost always it annihilates woman."[16] Germaine Greer suggests, "if independence is a necessary concomitant of freedom, woman must not marry."[17] Kate Millett feels that marriage reduces the status of woman to a mere object for decoration and a tool to be used for man's sexual gratification. Deshpande's protagonists are, no doubt, victims of this unequal power structure in marriage, but in all her novels she shows how one can rise above such injustice and lead a meaningful existence. In the end, her protagonists almost always strive to make their marriages work. As J. Bhavani observes: "This is not a negative but a realistic end to the novels. Deshpande upholds marriage as the backbone of society, what is stifling is the persona of the wife and not the institution of marriage."[18]

We may say that Deshpande's views coincide with modern

feminist thought which has changed much since the radical feminism of the 1960s. In her book, *The Feminist Mystique*, which took American society by storm, Betty Friedan challenged the universal belief that a woman should find contentment in motherhood and domesticity. Two decades later, Betty Friedan in her book, *The Second Stage*, says that humanity can survive only if women make certain compromises. She suggests that women should pursue some meaningful activity within marriage in order to find happiness and contentment in their lives.

But it is obvious that Deshpande never intends to subscribe to the views of any feminist. Her characters, though urban and educated, are firmly rooted in India with the weight of centuries of tradition and culture behind them. In his essay, "Problematising Feminism," Jaidev says: "It is very necessary for us to have feminism in this country but then this feminism has to be authentic, rooted and context-bound. One does not mind if our feminists are not too clever or good at quoting western critics or weaving intricate post-structuralist cobwebs."[19]

Deshpande may not be a formal feminist in the strict sense of the word, but it must also be observed that feminism can mean different things to different people. Arshia Sattar in her thought-provoking article on the position of the feminist movement at present observes: "Feminism is no longer a single voice that speaks for all women irrespective of creed and colour. It is, rather, a 'rainbow coalition' of rights, desires, agendas, struggles, victories. Not all issues apply to all women, our battles need not be the same and, more and more, we tend to speak for ourselves rather than for all of us."[20]

Whether or not she is a feminist, Shashi Deshpande has definitely carved a niche for herself in voicing the thoughts and feelings of the educated, urban middle-class woman. Though Kamala Markandaya, Anita Desai and Nayantara Sahgal have all ventured into this area of writing, none has pursued it with the single-mindedness and relentlessness of Deshpande. She has "never sworn allegiance to what we normally think of as feminist theories of the novel and yet or maybe because of the absence of this overt avowal, she has succeeded in providing her readers with a perspective which is simultaneously, truly individualistic and feminine."[21] She is basically interested in the issues, not just pertaining to women, but extended to all humanity. Despite her disapproval, she has been considered a 'woman writer,' rather than a writer who deals with "human issues" which are "of interest to all humanity." This has been made clear by Shashi Deshpande herself most recently in her article 'Of Concerns, of Anxieties,' where she says:

> I have been put into the slot of woman writer, my writing has been categorized as 'writing about women' or 'feminist' writing. In this process, much in it has been missed. I have been denied the place and dignity of a writer who is dealing with issues that are human issues, of interest to all humanity. (100)

From this it is clear that Shashi Deshpande is more humanist than a womanist or a feminist.

NOTES

1. Rani Dharkar, "Marriage as Purdah: Fictional Rendering of a Social Reality," *Margins of Erasure: Purdah in the Sub-Continental Novel in English*, ed. Jasbir Jain and Amina Amin (New Delhi: Sterling, 1995), 50.
2. Nicholas Abercrombie, Stephen Hill and Bryan S. Turner, *Dictionary of Sociology* (Harmondsworth: Penguin, 1984), 127.
3. Ephesians, 5:22, *The Bible*.
4. *Manusmriti*, V, 154, *Manav Dharm Shastra*, trans. and ed. Graves Chamnen Haughtoll, Vol. III (New Delhi: Cosmo, 1982).
5. Susan Wadley, "Women and the Hindu Tradition," *Women in Indian Society*, ed. Rehana Ghadially (New Delhi: Sage, 1988), 29.
6. Shashi Deshpande, *That Long Silence* (New Delhi: Penguin, 1989), 32.
7. Sudhir Kakar, "Feminine Identity in India," *Women in Indian Society*, 49.